The psychology of second language learning

The psychology of second language learning

PAPERS FROM THE SECOND
INTERNATIONAL CONGRESS OF
APPLIED LINGUISTICS
CAMBRIDGE, 8–12 SEPTEMBER 1969

EDITED BY
PAUL PIMSLEUR
Professor of Education and Romance Languages,
State University of New York, Albany

AND

TERENCE QUINN
Lecturer in French, Monash University

CAMBRIDGE
AT THE UNIVERSITY PRESS 1971

Published by the Syndics of the Cambridge University Press
Bentley House, 200 Euston Road, London NW1 2DB
American Branch: 32 East 57th Street, New York, N.Y.10022

Library of Congress Catalogue Card Number: 75–173811

ISBN: 0 521 08236 6

Printed in Great Britain
at the University Printing House, Cambridge
(Brooke Crutchley, University Printer)

Contents

1634949

CONTENTS

vi

Preface

The congress at which these papers were presented came at an important time in the history of language teaching: it was the end of a decade, and the end of an era; some would even say that it was a moment of crisis. At least in the United States, the beginning of the 1960s had been marked by a buoyant spirit of confidence in the exciting times that lay ahead for the language teaching profession: there was great public interest in foreign language teaching, abundant government support, and hopeful confidence in the rapidly developing audio-lingual movement. By the end of the decade, all this had changed: foreign language courses were faring badly as students demanded 'relevance', and many institutions abandoned foreign language requirements; government funds became scarcer, and a mood of self-questioning became perceptible throughout the profession. The audio-lingual movement had succeeded admirably in bringing an emphasis on the spoken language into the classroom, and in making teachers aware of the complexity of the language learning task; yet, precisely because of these achievements, new problems had arisen which needed a broader and stronger theoretical framework than audio-lingualism could provide.

There are some grounds for believing that the new theoretical constructs and new insights we need may come from the field of psychology. We may be moving away from what has perhaps been an excessive preoccupation with the linguistic bases of language teaching. Previously dazzled by the complicated techniques and hermetic language of the linguists, we now see their contribution in better perspective: a useful adjunct, particularly to the textbook writer, but still begging the central question: how can the material, however expertly analysed, be presented to the student so that he will develop foreign language competence? This is clearly a question for psychology to answer. We would suggest that the focus of our enquiries must move from the language to the learner, from the material to the person who is to absorb it. The more we understand about how students learn, the better we shall teach.

The papers in this collection indicate that there is as yet no common approach to the psychology of second language learning. The contributors were invited to choose their own topics, and to deal with any aspect of the general subject; no attempt was made to impose any unifying theme. Nonetheless, it is interesting to note that certain dominant themes do emerge, and these merit some comment. They are signs of where the language teaching profession is heading, of trends that might well become the leading ideas of the 1970s.

One is struck by a new focus on the individual learner as the central element in the complex process of second language acquisition: the unpredictable individual learner receives far more attention in these papers than do methods, materials or theories. Our students, we are reminded, come to us with amazingly different gifts and goals; we must accept them as they are if we wish to teach them a language successfully. Several contributors exhibit this attitude of optimistic pragmatism towards the individual learner, and there is considerable interest in allowing for, and indeed paying close attention to the individual's strategies of learning. This is a far cry from the rigid control of methods and materials that was characteristic of the last decade. We are beginning to realize that we cannot totally regulate or predict what strategy will work for each individual learner. Thus, we see a far greater openness to suggestions that would have been considered outlandish a few years ago. Newmark outlines an approach which simply provides the individual student with access to the language in the form of a native speaker and authentic reading material, and lets him go about learning largely in his own way. Dato studies in detail the self-generated strategy of a child, the path or programme of learning he follows as he moves towards bilingualism. Selinker suggests a new set of theoretical constructs for analysing and guiding our observation of the student's learning strategies, and Carton suggests that techniques of 'inferencing' may play a very important part in these strategies. This interest in the learning strategy of the individual student opens up an exciting new world of enquiry: how does a learner go about acquiring the language if we do not insist on his using our method? How successful is he? Why – in Valette's terms – does he fail to achieve mastery learning? Tolerance, and even encouragement of vastly differing learner strategies may well be a characteristic of the language teaching profession in the future.

On the other hand, fruitful empirical research into the adult learner's strategies may depend upon restatements of theory. Sapon suggests that a more thorough analysis of language learning as a process of acquiring

viii

verbal behaviour may have a great deal to offer, despite the current unpopularity of this orientation among linguists. Reibel, working from an entirely different perspective, thoroughly investigates the theoretical concepts we use to interpret the facts of adult language learning, and suggests some restatements that might well bear fruit in empirical studies such as those described by Titone. Some interesting evidence already emerges from the empirical studies conducted by Mueller within the theoretical framework of current methodologies.

Several authors in this collection suggest that during the 1960s we neglected some aspects of language skill: they point to a growing awareness that the so-called 'receptive' skills of listening and reading are vastly more complex than many of us had imagined. Adherence to the basic principles of a Listen–Speak–Read–Write sequence has served many teachers well, but we need to examine the individual components of the sequence more closely. Nida's experience suggests that there may be little connection between a person's level of achievement in listening comprehension and his skill in speech: complete ease of comprehension may be accompanied by a total inability to say anything. Belasco points to several years' experience of the opposite phenomenon: participants at National Defense Education Act language institutes were able to develop a certain kind of speaking ability, and yet had very great difficulty in understanding normal speech. We tend to assume that listening and reading are basically similar in being 'receptive' skills, but Goodman, in analysing the essential aspects of the act of reading, points to several respects in which the two skills are very different. All of this tends to suggest that listening comprehension may be the key fundamental skill that has not been adequately understood. It is to this problem that Rivers addresses herself: in a theoretical analysis, she examines in depth the exact nature of the listening act; then, in an outline of the practical applications of available theory, she explores means of training students in listening comprehension by leading them through successive stages of increasing complexity. Mear gives a full account of the methods she used to train young children to respond accurately to a quite extensive 'receptive repertoire'. (During the congress, James J. Asher also presented a film illustrating his work in teaching comprehension by the technique of 'total physical response'.) Friedman and Johnson also address themselves to the analysis of listening behaviour: in their work on rate-controlled speech they have investigated the quite extraordinary human capacity for processing speech even when it is considerably 'distorted', and have demonstrated that this capacity can be further developed by training. Further work on the analysis of comprehension will probably be one of the main preoccupations of our profession in the next few years.

Finally, one detects a desire to bring our students into closer contact with 'real' language, with language as it is used in the real world by people successfully communicating with each other. Indeed, Nida suggests that the study of language learners once they have left the unreal world of the classroom will give us insights not available from any other source. Oller argues that the linguistic analysis on which our teaching is based must include situational language, language at work as part of the act of communication. Obrecht stresses the need for us to be constantly aware of the 'mutual effect between language and environment', and decries our neglect of this aspect of language use in our classrooms: his suggestion of a language simulator to bring something closer to actual language experience back into our programmes is an exciting earnest of things to come. The experience of language in use is the key feature of Newmark's programme, and Belasco equally demands that 'real' language find a proper place in our courses. 'Real' language is essentially language used to convey meaning from one person to another and Oller argues convincingly that we should be far more aware of this communicative function of language, and should pay much more attention to the *meaning* of the language material we use in our classes. His position is further supported by those who, like Estacio, believe that language teachers have a good deal to learn from developments in cognitive psychology. Certainly, considerable stress on extra-linguistic information – Oller's 'pragmatics' – is essential to a theory of second language learning.

Beyond these leading ideas, the contribution of each writer is far richer than any of the themes we have suggested. Many stimulating ideas defy categorization, as is inevitable at a moment of basic re-evaluation, when there is as yet no commonality of approach to the psychology of language learning. The approaches suggested in these papers are indeed disparate: tiny, incremental, programmed steps contrast with global, self-directed, absorptive 'sunburn' techniques; cognition vies with habit formation; and Gestalt psychology competes with stimulus-response theory. (To our great regret, there is no contribution on the biology of learning: there was a paper offered on neurolinguistics, but finally its writer was unable to attend.)

There are thus many seminal ideas, rather than directly applicable solutions proposed in these papers. We would hope that this is the strength of the collection, as it was of the congress. A similar collection ten years ago might have offered confident recipes for success: the writers of the present papers are noticeably less inclined to advocate a single 'method', being aware of the complexity of second language behaviour; what they have to offer are hints of new directions based on a half-century of psychological research and reflection. In the aggregate they suggest that we are making some progress in the analysis of that complex human phenomenon known as foreign language learning.

PAUL PIMSLEUR
TERENCE QUINN

August
1971

I   *The feasibility of learning a second language in an artificial unicultural situation*

SIMON BELASCO

Just ten years ago this month, in September 1959, I completed teaching the applied linguistics course for French, Spanish, and German secondary school teachers at the Foreign Language Summer Institute held at Colgate University. This institute was one of the first three or four summer language institutes in 1959 established under the provisions of the National Defense Act of 1958. During the decade that followed, thousands of secondary school teachers in hundreds of NDEA institutes in the United States and abroad were indoctrinated in audiolingual techniques and methodology designed to make them better teachers of foreign languages.

I consider myself especially privileged to have taught applied linguistics courses in five summer institutes in the States, one summer institute in Besançon, France, and two Academic-Year French Institutes at Pennsylvania State University, which I personally directed in 1960–1 and 1961–2. I mention these facts not so much to lend authority to the statements I am about to make, as to stress the vantage point I have had to observe both secondary school and university teachers performing as students and as instructors of foreign languages. My participation in the NDEA programs proved to be a most revealing experience for me. It certainly was the major factor in shaping my thinking on second language learning.

In the first version of the *Manual and anthology of applied linguistics: General Section, French, German, Italian, Russian, Spanish,* I proposed a four-fold approach to teaching a second language utilizing the techniques of (1) formal contrast, (2) structural marking, (3) syntactic functive analysis (subsequently renamed tagmemics), and (4) transformation grammar.[1] The manual was distributed free of charge by the government to every participant attending a NDEA institute in the summer of 1960. It was expressly designed to explain the rationale behind the New Key Approach to foreign language teaching, and it stressed the systematic and intensive application of the aforementioned four techniques to the acquisition of audiolingual skills.

Ten years ago the concept of the structurally seeded dialogue – reinforced by substitution drills, correlation drills, and transformation drills – was virtually unknown to most high school and college teachers of foreign language. Most teachers had been brought up in the grammar–translation tradition and were very much aware that they lacked certain language skills when they became institute participants. It was expected that after each participant underwent a period of indoctrination and training, he would acquire the necessary language and teaching skills by the very methods and techniques he was to use later with his students when he returned to the teaching situation.

Many participants found the linguist's jargon – if not his rationale – more cryptic than enlightening. The experience proved to be traumatic – especially in methodology classes where participants were asked to demonstrate New Key techniques before their peers. Many dreaded running through a drill sequence, not because they were against the audiolingual approach but because they did not feel competent enough to do pattern practice either as teachers or as students.

Despite all the initial reaction, disappointment, and frustration, New Key procedures did catch on and are very much in evidence in the United States today both in high school and college foreign language classrooms. There is a genuine interest and willingness on the part of foreign language teachers to incorporate audiolingual techniques into their programs. They are not, however, unaware of recent statements which appear to question the validity of New Key procedures – including the value of pattern practice and the contribution of linguistics and psychology to second language learning – that are being made by some of the earliest and strongest supporters of the audiolingual approach.[2]

For the past few years I have been saying that even if a foreign language student acquired one hundred percent of the subject matter taught by

[1] Pursuant to a contract with the United States government, two versions of the manual appeared: see Belasco (1960 and 1961). A revised version of the General and French section has recently been published: see Belasco and Valdman (1968).

[2] Valdman (1965), p. 297, and Belasco (1966 and 1967).

any known method – traditional or audiolingual – he would get no further than he is now: on a plateau that leads nowhere.[1]

These remarks are not to be construed as being anti-audiolingual or counter-revolutionary. In fact they derive from direct experience with programs where the audiolingual method has enjoyed no small measure of success.

At the end of the 1960–1 Penn State Academic-Year French Institute, I was rudely jolted by the realization that it is possible to develop so-called 'speaking' ability and yet be virtually incompetent in under-standing the spoken language. To illustrate, participants at the Penn State Institute took the uniform pre-institute and post-institute Modern Language Association Proficiency Tests prescribed for every institute participant.[2] A comparison of the Penn State average speaking scores with those of All-French Institute participants – which included all-French academic year institutes, French summer institutes abroad, and French summer institutes in the States reveals the results given in Table 1.

TABLE I. *1960–1 MLA speaking scores*

	Penn State average	All-Institute average
Pre-test	171.0476	178.3738
Post-test	218.3684	181.5057
Improvement	47.3208	3.1301

The tests were not graded by the institutes themselves, but were graded off-campus by MLA specialists at a central point. The Penn State average of 47+ points compared with the All-French Institute national average of 3+ points (which included the Penn State score) seemed to justify the enormous emphasis placed on step-incremented drills using face-to-face contact and electronic devices, which were major features of the Penn State program. (Let no one deceive himself that we considered this type of 'vocalizing' as real linguistic performance or conversational ability.)

Nonetheless, when the scores involving the listening, reading, and writing skills were compared with the high score for speaking, the results were disappointing.

[1] Belasco (1967), p. 82.　　　　[2] Belasco (1965).

TABLE 2. *1960–1 MLA four skill scores* (*Penn State French Institute*)

Mean post-test/pre-test difference			
1. Speaking	47.3208	3. Reading	4.3913
2. Listening	2.5039	4. Writing	2.0435

The nationwide scores in French for the last three skills did not differ substantially from the Penn State scores. What surprised me most was that a marked improvement in verbal facility by MLA standards was not accompanied by a significant improvement in listening comprehension.

Even at that time I strongly suspected that the accepted sequence of emphasizing 'listening, speaking, reading, and writing' in that order was only being observed superficially. Not enough stress was being placed on listening comprehension, i.e. not enough opportunity was given the student to 'overhear natural conversations between second and third parties.' In other words participants were learning to audio-comprehend certain specific dialogues and drills taught by native speakers – but could not understand spoken French out of context in the mouths of native speakers.

In 1963, I was most optimistic about the prospect of teaching foreign languages by linear and branching techniques utilized in programmed learning.[1] As chairman of the Working Committee on Listening and Speaking of the 1963 Northeast Conference on the Teaching of Foreign Languages, I suggested that a carefully integrated series of step-incremented drills consisting of some 50,000 carefully selected structural features might be conceivably equivalent to the amount of structure internalized by the average native speaker of a given language. By shifting the emphasis from covering a relatively indefinite amount of language within a definite period of time to assimilating a definite amount of language within a relatively indefinite period of time, more effective results could be realized in a team-teaching situation – involving self-evaluation techniques and self-pacing procedures taught 'live' and/or in the language laboratory.

The method proposed a sixteen-week semester system divided into eight two-week learning units. Ideally, each teacher of a team of four instructors would be in charge of two of these learning units. Each student was to be progressively shifted from one two-week unit to the

[1] Belasco (1963*a* and *b*).

4

next higher unit *only if* he made an achievement score of 90% or better. Upon completing the course, every student would receive an A since that is the grade normally given for 90% achievement. Of course, not all students would necessarily finish the first semester's work at the end of sixteen weeks. If six sections of twenty students each – or a total of 120 students – began the semester at the same time, at the end of sixteen weeks they might be spread over the program as shown in Table 3:

TABLE 3. *Spread of students at the end of sixteen weeks*

Number of the unit (two-week segment)	I	II	III	IV	V	VI	VII	VIII
Instructor	A	B	C	D	D	C	B	A
Number of pupils in class	2	3	5	8	10	22	30	40
		9 a.m. class				10 a.m. class		

The figure of 50,000 selected features is, of course, arbitrary, and we do not suggest that it be taken seriously. In the ordinary classroom situation, students may be exposed to a barrage of language that exceeds 50,000 structural features. Yet each student assimilates chunks of this structure in varying degrees at the completion of the foreign language course. The team-teaching method suggested here exercises far more control over what the student assimilates. But the nagging question still remains: What will the student actually be assimilating? Do the structure-dependent operations a student performs in any foreign language course – audiolingual or otherwise – reflect a fair sample of the 'real' language? In other words, even if he internalizes all of the 50,000 structural features, what does this mean in terms of the actual syntactic, semantic, and phonological features necessary for the acquisition of linguistic competence in a foreign language? The assumption that one or more courses presently exist that do contain a fair sample of the 'real' language is certainly naïve and unrealistic. Nonetheless it would be revealing to experiment with the team-teaching procedure despite the lack of ideal materials.

The chances are good that a modified version of this technique will be used at Penn State in the near future. Certain informal pilot studies seem to indicate, however, that this technique will not work *with contrived materials alone;* that is, the current variety of audiolingual materials or grammar–translation materials must be supplemented with 'live' materials before the gap between *basic* foreign language performance and *real* foreign language performance can be bridged.

We have repeatedly advocated the use of live or 'controlled' materials in second language learning.[1] It is possible for contrived materials to develop a student's awareness of the set of possible forms making up the sound system and the morphophonemic system. They can develop a 'state of expectancy' for basic grammatical relations and features, e.g. concord, case, tense, aspect, mood, etc. On the other hand, controlled materials are transitional materials that make use of *live* written texts (novels, stories, newspaper articles) and recorded or taped texts (radio and televised broadcasts, interviews, sound track of films) and contribute to the linguistic competence of the learner by enlarging the range of awareness for variations in linguistic form, complex syntactic constructions, semantic differences in vocabulary, and differences of cultural concept and cultural emphasis.[2]

Controlled materials are introduced *after the contrived materials have supposedly taught the basic language* and are designed to develop the so-called 'passive' skills: listening and reading. They are bilingual materials containing English equivalents of foreign language texts that teach listening comprehension and reading by contrastive analysis. Grammar is taught live from the novels and sound tracks themselves, not from 'canned' textbooks.

Contrived materials are based on the logical assumptions of pedagogues, methodologists, and textbook writers and have little, if any, empirical justification. The concept of *scope* (whereby the student gets the overall 'big picture') *and sequence* (whereby grammatical principles are taught in logical steps and supposedly contain the grammatical constraints necessary to ensure correct analogizing) is as old as the profession of foreign language teaching and is a myth. If *contrived materials alone* have not succeeded until now, what assurance is there that they will ever succeed? We wish to emphasize the word 'alone' since contrived materials, programmed scientifically, represent an excellent means of teaching *basic* phonetic, morphophonemic, and syntactic structure.

There are tremendous individual differences among students. They

---

[1] See references cited in previous footnotes, as well as Belasco (1968, 1969, and forthcoming *a* and *b*).

[2] For a discussion of cultural concept and cultural emphasis, see Belasco (1967).

simply do not learn a second language in the same way. They probably do not learn their native language in the same way. What is a pedagogically logical step for one student may – if introduced too soon – prove a source of interference for another student. Foreign language materials, contrived as they are, never take into consideration individual differences among students. And even if they did we simply do not know enough about language structure or cognitive processes to know what should go into the materials or how the student should go about learning them. Those who do manage to learn a foreign language do so not because of the system but in spite of it – and they make up less than five per cent of the students enrolled in foreign language courses.

A child learning his native language hears false starts and stops, hemming and hawing, baby talk, distorted speech, non-linguistic noise – and from this state of chaos characteristic of the so-called primary linguistic data, he develops linguistic competence, i.e. he constructs a grammar of his native language.

Controlled listening and reading materials have built-in self-pacing and self-evaluating characteristics and seem to contain the necessary primary data with just those semantic, syntactic, and phonological features that are lacking in contrived materials. In other words, whatever is missing from current pedagogical materials appears to be contained in the live materials, and it is these materials that enable our little black boxes (the language acquisition mechanism) to develop a degree of linguistic competence that may some day lead to the degree of linguistic performance characterizing the true creative aspect of language use.

Performance on tests in a regular language course does not necessarily correlate with performance on standardized tests. There is evidence that – within a given achievement group in first and second year college French – a higher correlation exists between performance on standardized tests and the length of time a student spends studying a foreign language.

For example, an investigation was conducted this past year at Penn State to examine the effectiveness of bilingual reading materials in teaching Reading Comprehension to 127 students in an intermediate course in college French.[1] The reading experiment was conducted for

---

[1] Parent (1969). The student was also asked on the weekly tests to write an English translation of the answers he selected. Tests were scored a second time and correct answers to the multiple-choice items were counted only when accompanied by a translation which indicated that the student had

one hour a week over a ten-week period. All of the students had been studying French with the same contrived materials for twenty weeks when the experiment began. The students in each of seven sections were divided into three equalized groups according to scores made on Form LA of the MLA Cooperative Classroom Reading Test in French. Group A used all-French reading materials and a French-to-English glossary. Group B used parallel column English–French (bilingual) reading materials and the same glossary. Group C used the same materials as Group B with the self-pacing option of listening to the French text on tape. At the end of each reading hour, all materials were collected and the students took a fifteen-minute multiple-choice test written entirely in French.

On the weekly objective tests students in Groups B and C received significantly higher scores than students in Group A. However, at the end of the ten-week experimental period, there was no observed improvement in any group in 'reading comprehension' as measured by the MLA Cooperative Test.

TABLE 4

	Means on weekly objective tests	MLA Coop Reading Test group means	
		Pre-test Form LA	Post-test Form LB
Group A (unilingual text)	66.05	30.41	30.72
Group B (bilingual text)	83.96	30.22	29.76
Group C (bilingual text plus recording)	84.28	31.40	31.19

It may be that in order for the second language learner to make a significant improvement in the reading skill – even with controlled materials – he must reach a certain threshold, i.e. there is a critical bound on the amount of time a student must be exposed to reading in

understood the meaning of the answer. When these modified scores were tabulated, the differences between Group A on the one hand and Groups B and C on the other were even greater. Very little difference was found to exist, however, between Groups B and C.

the foreign language, and this will certainly vary with each student. (Moreover, it is doubtful that the MLA Cooperative Reading Tests – which reflect a heavy vocabulary bias – actually sample the reading comprehension skill as it exists in the real world.)

The question now must be asked as to whether a foreign language *can* be acquired in a unicultural, artificial situation involving the classroom and the language laboratory. As yet, no one can really answer this question. Studies of foreign language acquisition use elementary and intermediate language students as subjects – and this despite the fact that most foreign language teachers, graduate students, and undergraduate majors have not as yet developed the necessary foreign language skills. Any experimental program should at least be tried out first with foreign language majors.[1] If it succeeds with them, then the method can be applied 'downward' to non-majors, first with advanced students, then intermediate students, and finally elementary students. How far 'down' one can go will depend on the extent to which a foreign language program is geared exclusively to second language acquisition. The environmental conditions for learning a foreign language are not suitable within existing departmental programs dominated by linguistic, literary, educational, or psychological philosophies. Nothing is wrong with preparing foreign language majors for careers in literature, linguistics, or foreign language teaching – but not at the expense of those students who desire to major primarily, if not exclusively, in understanding, speaking, reading and writing one or more foreign languages.

If a second language can be learned in a classroom, it will come as a result of research performed on, and by, future foreign language majors, who may not necessarily become foreign language teachers. Candidates for a 'meaningful' BA degree in Language Proficiency will be concerned with developing near native proficiency in the four skills. Candidates for a 'meaningful' PhD degree in Language Acquisition will devote themselves to research that will enable undergraduate students to acquire listening, reading, writing, and real speaking in an artificial, unicultural situation. This does not preclude research in the related disciplines, but it does mean that the acquisition of foreign language skills must take precedence over any linguistically, esthetically, or educationally oriented considerations. If materials can be designed so that individual differences among students are taken into consideration, it may be possible to define a foreign language goal in terms of student achievement rather

[1] Belasco (forthcoming *b*).

9

than in terms of academic year blocks. The acquisition of foreign language skills should take place in the elementary and secondary schools, making it unnecessary to extend this function to the university.

BIBLIOGRAPHY

Belasco, Simon (ed.). *Manual and anthology of applied linguistics: General Section, French, German, Italian, Russian, Spanish.* University Park, Pennsylvania: Nittany Press, 1960.
Applied linguistics: French, German, Italian, Russian, Spanish. 5 vols. Boston: D. C. Heath, 1961.
'Structural drills and the refinement principle.' In *Structural drill and the language laboratory. International Journal of American Linguistics*, publication 27, vol. 29, no. 2, pt. 3 (April 1963), 19–36 (1963*a*).
Belasco, Simon, *et al.* 'The continuum: listening and speaking.' In *Reports of the Working Committees, 1963 Northeast Conference on the Teaching of Foreign Languages* (1963*b*).
Belasco, Simon. 'Nucleation and the audio-lingual approach.' *The Modern Language Journal,* **49** (1965), 482–91.
'Structure plus meaning equals language proficiency.' *The Florida FL Reporter,* **4**, no. 3 (Spring 1966), 13–14.
'The plateau or the case for comprehension: the 'concept' approach.' *The Modern Language Journal,* **51** (1967), 82–6.
'Surface structure and deep structure in English.' *Midway,* **3** (Autumn 1968), 111–23.
'Toward the acquisition of linguistic competence: from contrived to controlled materials.' *The Modern Language Journal,* **53** (1969), 185–205.
'The foreign language teacher in search of values.' In *Dimensions 1969: Proceedings of the 1969 Southern Conference on Language Teaching* (forthcoming *a*).
'Where is programmed language instruction most effective?' In *Proceedings of the 1969 Kentucky Foreign Language Conference* (forthcoming *b*).
Belasco, Simon, and Valdman, Albert. *Applied linguistics and the teaching of French.* University Park, Pennsylvania: Nittany Press, 1968.
Parent, Pierre Paul. 'Toward the nucleation stage: an investigation of the effectiveness of three methods of developing reading comprehension in a college course in Intermediate French.' Diss., Pennsylvania State University, 1969.
Valdman, Albert. *The implementation and evaluation of a multiple-credit self-instructional elementary French course, Final Report.* Bloomington, Ind.: Indiana University, 1965.

2 A minimal language-teaching program

LEONARD D. NEWMARK

INTRODUCTION

It is frequently asserted that the first step in designing an educational program, is to make an exact analysis of what we want the student to know; then, using available teaching techniques and technologies, we merely apply our knowledge of educational engineering to bring about the desired end: the student knows that which we had decided to teach him. I have argued elsewhere that in the case of language teaching,[1] such a first step is presently unavailable to us, and that as language-teaching engineers we do better to base the design of language-teaching programs on our disciplined observation of the conditions under which learners do in fact learn languages than to base them on the detailed, explicit, partial characterizations of languages we have gained so far from modern linguistics. Eventually, if and as we achieve a substantive theory of language development integrating semantic and pragmatic (as well as intonational and paralinguistic) components into a general linguistic theory that accounts also for syntactic and phonological well-formation, we may be able to derive increasingly more efficient language-teaching strategies. At present, however, we should be cognizant of the extent of our ignorance as well as the extent of our knowledge, and our programs should present the student the opportunity to learn the language, even if we have no 'scientific' basis yet for organizing that opportunity for him.

GENERAL GOALS

At the University of California in San Diego, we have tried to start out with a language program that consists of just such a set of opportunities.

[1] Newmark (1964a and b, 1966, 1967), and Newmark and Reibel (1968).

Starting at a brand-new university with no established faculty and curriculum, we were free to make a fresh attempt to incorporate into our program only those elements that could be motivated on the basis of a minimal theory of language acquisition, without having to reconcile conflicting superstitious views of experienced teachers about 'what works' in language teaching. We were encouraged to experiment in developing a whole, integrated language program for the university rather than to patch together a set of courses and materials out of the existing practices of individual teachers. Our constraints were that our new program could cost no more than existing language programs on other campuses of the University of California and that our students could spend no more time per week (roughly twelve to fifteen hours) in total language study than they would spend for their other courses at the university. In addition, we imposed the requirement on the program that within sixty weeks, and preferably thirty, it enable *any* student to demonstrate the ability to carry on ordinary conversation and do everyday, non-professional reading in the language; we also imposed on ourselves the requirement that our course should contribute directly to the liberal education of the university student: for example, we would consider it an insufficient result if our students could converse, however well, in the language but be improperly prepared to take courses in the literature of the language, and insufficient also if he had learned to use a language but had learned nothing *about* that language and about the nature of language in general.

MINIMAL THEORY

Our plan was to initiate a program that provided only the known minimal necessities at first, and to incorporate additional features into the program only as these could individually be demonstrated to increase the speed at which competence was gained.

As a point of departure, we assumed that no element of a language-teaching program could be necessary if successful first and second language learners had done without it in gaining their proficiency. It followed from this assumption that we could eliminate the favorite features of modern applied linguistics from our program: preparatory contrastive analysis of native and target languages to isolate problem areas; and, corresponding pattern drills of all kinds – phonological, morphological, and syntactic. We also assumed that no combination of elements could be sufficient if unsuccessful language students had been exposed to that combination without gaining the ability to use the language. On these grounds, we rejected courses organized around standard language textbooks, all of which in practice seemed to us to yield large numbers of students who, at best, were well prepared to *start* learning to use the language. We adopted the common-sense, but then heretical view that the best preparation for learning to use a language was observation of the language in use by others and experience in using the language oneself.

To provide students the opportunity to gain the skill of conversing in the language, we would arrange to have other people speak the language with them; to provide them the opportunity for learning to read in the language, we would supply books and newspapers written in the language. Just such minimal opportunities, we knew, have been sufficient for hundreds of millions of other people – for the most part children – to learn to speak and read languages with native fluency. To provide students with information about language in general, and about the language they were studying in particular, we gave occasional lectures on linguistics and suggested some traditional grammatical descriptions for them to read.

CONVERSATION

Now came the additions and refinements to increase the efficiency of the program, additions and refinements adapted to the particular requirements and constraints of our givens. For example, because ours were university students expected to learn educated adult varieties of the language, we specified that their immediate models (the people who would speak the language with them in our classes) be educated native or quasi-native adult speakers rather than specifying, say, three-year old children or professional teachers (who on other possible theories of language acquisition might be claimed to be superior as language tutors). As models we were able to employ for the most part graduate and undergraduate students at the university – with the double benefit of keeping our budget for wages low and increasing the level of financial support for foreign students on our campus. Within our budget, we could provide even these models to students for only three hours a week if we insisted, as we did, that the meetings with the models would be conversational in tone (no more than eight students per model). Given this severe three-hour a week limitation on the student's opportunity to observe the language, we decided to provide tape recorded versions of dialogues for the students to listen to outside of class. Because recordings can easily be listened to with both ears open – in one ear and out the other – we added progressively more detailed instructions for attentive listening to ensure that laboratory time was optimally used. Because listening without understanding does not constitute *observation* of language use but mere exposure to language sounds, we provided scripts in English to enable the student to understand the dialogues.

Like children, adults in the process of acquiring a language normally fall considerably short of native-like performance in their early performance attempts. Unlike children, the self-sufficient adult learner may continue indefinitely to tune out feedback from other speakers that would induce him spontaneously to adjust details of his performance to match that of his model's: in other words, adults speak with non-native accents (exhibit interference) longer than children do. To induce the adult to tune in the feedback and thus increase the efficiency of his observation, a number of techniques have been tried by language teachers: e.g. discrimination exercises using a human or laboratory model, introduced before, during, or after contact with real (i.e. used) language; phonological (including detailed phonetic) explanations; simple repetition of recorded or live model performance with or without student performance, with or without invited comparison of student and model performance; pre-program training in production of nonsense syllables; pre-program training in production of student's native language pronounced with the accent of the target language, etc.

In planning our language program, I was struck by the fact that the common element in all these techniques – each of which has its loyal proponents who report 'success' for their method – is simply that in each case the student's attention is directed at what he is hearing, that he is not permitted to be casual about the feedback. I further noticed that even 'bad' training programs, e.g. pronunciation classes in which the phonological explanation is inept, or those in which the teacher called attention to the wrong element for correction, often produce students who improve as much as those in 'good' programs. As a minimal basis for the improvement of surface details, then, we adopted a set of unprogrammed attention-inducing techniques. Specifically, in their conversation sessions with students, our models are instructed to have the student speak in repeated unison with the model the phrases and sentences to be improved. Subject to empirical falsification, I would claim that the concentration required to keep in time with the model provides all the attention needed for the feedback to be effective. Similarly, for his laboratory study of dialogues, the student is instructed to listen repeatedly to each section of speech (using laboratory machines capable of rapid and instantly controllable repeat) until he can speak in easy unison with the tape model.

READING

Careful observation of cases of successful versus unsuccessful language students suggests that it is not so important to prevent contamination of one language by another as it is essential that the student experience meaning in the language examples to which he is exposed. In the case of reading, our program took advantage of the students' literacy in their own language to provide efficient visual aids to understanding, generally in the form of running glosses in English, rather than oral ones, in the form of teachers' in-class explanations (in English or in the language) of what the foreign language version says. For the sake of efficiency, we decided to eliminate the time-consuming exercise of student thumbs in using dictionaries and end glosses, and either adopted reading materials already provided with running glosses or adapted reading materials for our use by writing our own running glosses. In some cases (French, Russian, Spanish, Italian), we found elementary programmed or quasi-programmed readers that could provide non-aversive introductions to reading with understanding in the language; our comparison of classes exposed to such graded materials versus those exposed to ungraded but fully glossed materials from the beginning is not yet meaningful because of the plethora of unmatched variables so usual in educational research, but at the moment no grossly apparent difference has appeared.

ORGANIZATION OF TIME

The distribution of time among various learning activities in the program was difficult to establish as a matter of principle, and our final distribution was determined almost as much by considerations of budget and scheduling problems as by consideration of educational priorities. In the end, we apportioned the twelve hours a week of student time we had at our disposal as follows:

Three one-hour conversational sessions in small, homo-   3 hours
geneous groups with a native speaker. Homogeneity
maximized by weekly redistribution of students among
groups.

One two-hour group conference with a graduate assistant   2
in linguistics. The assistant's duties are to discuss
language and language acquisition in general and to help
students find answers to questions about the phonology
and grammar of the particular language under study.

Three one-hour assignments in the language laboratory   3
with individually controlled tape-decks. In general, two
of the assignments are to learn or review specially written dialogues; one assignment is a self-instructional
question-answer program directly aimed at building up
student competence to answer, in class, detailed questions about assigned newspaper and book reading
assignments.

Two hours of extensive reading in the foreign language.   2
In order to encourage scanning and rapid reading,
assignments are purposely longer (10–20 pages) than
students can study cryptoanalytically, and examinations
on readings purposely encourage rapid sketchy reading.

One hour study of a conventional grammar book to learn   1
the traditional nomenclature for reference use in later
work with the language.

One hour reading in general linguistics or in the history of   1
civilization associated with the language under study.

Total student time   12 hours

RESULTS

As is usual in educational research, it is difficult not to misrepresent the
results of experiments. Either the experiment is carefully controlled
but so artificial that one overstates its implications in order to give his
conclusions the appearance of non-triviality, or the experiment is so
complex and has so many uncontrolled variables that the experimenter
is forced either to state his conclusion in terms of vague tendencies or to
pretend that he can tell which of the many variables involved were
crucial in yielding the observed results. I am uncomfortable with trivi-
alities and so our experimental conclusions fall into the category of
selective reportage of putative tendencies.

First and most important, by thirty weeks 37 per cent of the students
who begin their study of a language with us and participate at all in our
program do achieve all our intended goals, including the ability to hold

16

conversations in the language easily on random topics and to read ordinary written material with rapid comprehension.[1] By forty weeks, 50 per cent have achieved these goals; by fifty weeks, 80 per cent; and, by sixty weeks, 98 per cent. Although our program apportions relatively little time, both in class and out, to the teaching of reading, it is interesting to note that after thirty weeks (one academic year), our students consistently read better (as measured by the MLA Cooperative Foreign Language Reading Test scores and norms) than students elsewhere after two academic years.

Since our program was initiated in 1964, it has undergone constant refinement. In the first year, for example, we attempted to dispense with course-credits and grades for our program – those perennial bugaboos of American college education; but we discovered that our students were using the freedom from pressure we afforded them to study physics, mathematics, and La Jolla surfing conditions, rather than to do the reading and laboratory work we recommended. In the following years, we increasingly provided detailed feedback to the student in the form of familiar grades on daily examinations for each part of the recommended work, and have noted a corresponding, and sadly predictable, large increase in the success of the program in teaching languages. In the first three years of the program, we tried to predetermine the general substance of the conversational encounters with the models. At the students' and models' request, we have allowed these sessions more and more to follow the spontaneous interests of the participants, and now constrain only the general form of the sessions; for example, the model is not allowed to speak English in class, may provide only short *ad hoc* 'explanations' of grammatical and lexical items, must play the role of drama coach, helpful native-speaking supplier of correct forms, rather than play the lecturer and taskmaster; the students initiate and maintain the conversations, appealing to the model for help in saying what they want to say at the time they want to say it. In the reading part of our program, we plan, this year, to allow students to proceed at their own pace by allowing them considerable flexibility in taking examinations on each part of their assigned extensive reading. All of these modifications represent our attempts to increase the students' attentive participation in

[1] It would take me too far afield here to report on our technique for assessing these abilities. Let it suffice here to say that the determination is made by a jury of native speakers judging by direct sampling of the student's use of the language.

the program rather than our forced admission of inadequacy in our theoretical underpinnings.

There are many linguists who make the claim that the adults for whom our program is designed are incapable of forming native-like linguistic intuitions merely on the basis of structurally disorganized experiences of the language in use. I would claim that the results of even the program we have developed so far at least give the lie to that claim in its strongest form: our adult students in more or less time do learn to use it as natives learn to use the language: from experience with instances of language in use, and without benefit of the intellectual crutches adults allegedly need to help them limp along in learning a new language. Our experiments with various modifications of the basic minimal program suggest that the most dramatic improvement in students' abilities to use the language come from increasing our sophistication about how to induce students to attend to instances of language use rather than from increasing our sophistication about how to order the student's experience according to the supposed dictates of one or another linguistic analysis.

BIBLIOGRAPHY

Newmark, L. 'Grammatical theory and the teaching of English as a foreign language.' *The 1963 Conference Papers of the English Language Section of the National Association for Foreign Student Affairs*, March 1964 (*a*).
    Introduction to using American English. New York: Harper and Row, 1964 (*b*).
    'How not to interfere with language learning.' In *Language learning: The individual and the process. International Journal of American Linguistics*, publication 40, vol. 32, no. 1 (Jan. 1966), 77–83.
    'Principles of language acquisition.' *Proceedings of the 10th International Congress of Linguists.* Bucharest, Rumania, 1967.
Newmark, L., and Reibel, D. A. 'Necessity and sufficiency in language learning.' *IRAL*, **6** (1968), 145–64.

3 *The development of the Spanish verb phrase in children's second-language learning*

DANIEL P. DATO

Our understanding of children's native-language development has grown considerably in recent years as a result of psycholinguistic research done on many languages. Stated in terms of transformational grammar, findings in this type of investigation have shown that there are certain underlying structures and functions that are present in the languages analyzed thus far. These encouraging results in the search for universals in first-language development have led us to explore the existence of similar phenomena in the learning of a second language.

At the outset we would certainly recognize some of the striking differences between these two learning situations: with a child's first language, linguistic experience is a totally new phenomenon for him; in the case of learning a second language, the child already has at his disposal a whole set of linguistic concepts. From a motivational point of view, the circumstances surrounding the learning of a second language may be entirely different from those accompanying the learning of his first language. Some observers claim that because of these and other reasons second-language learning is precisely what we make it and, therefore, cannot provide us with scientific knowledge concerning human behavior as in the case of the inevitable, species-specific, process of first-language development. In this presentation we are taking the position that second language-learning research *can* be fruitful and that, under certain conditions, second-language learning will follow certain psycholinguistic patterns.

By using techniques similar to those in native-language investigations, we have studied the process by which several monolingual, American English-speaking children of different ages randomly learned Spanish while living in a natural environment, in Madrid during the period

1964–6. Even if we take into account such phenomena as interference and carryover from the first language, we can observe the development of second-language learning taking place in a fashion that is not only systematic but also highly accelerated.

RESEARCH DESIGN

In the interest of developing sound research techniques, we conducted a pilot study on one child during the first year. We chose as our subject our own son, who was four years and one month old when the family arrived in Madrid. So that we could maintain an accurate record of all speech samples for verification and discussion, we used only the data which we were able to record. The subject's speech was recorded twenty times for about thirty to forty minutes each session over a period of nine months, in a variety of stimulus situations: (1) with Spanish peers, ages four to eight, in supervised and unsupervised play both inside the home and outside; (2) with Spanish-speaking friends of parents; and (3) with a monolingual Spanish research assistant trained to elicit conversation by means of drawings, story-telling, and especially structured questions. It was extremely important, and at times difficult, to convey to the interviewer that he should not try to teach the child Spanish, but should aim to elicit language samples from him which were representative of his linguistic competence at a particular time. In order to encourage him to speak spontaneously, a special transmitting microphone was placed around the child's body, allowing him to move around unencumbered by wires. The utterances he produced were picked up by a radio receiver placed in another room and recorded onto a tape recorder connected by means of a patch cord. Our pilot study, which was continued during the second year, served as an important methodological testing ground for the next phase of our research.

Our group study during the second year was to provide data which represented significantly the second-language-learning behavior of a particular age level. We chose six children between the ages of five and one-half and six and one-half because we wanted subjects who: (1) had reached the point where they had mastered the basic rudiments of their native language – i.e. most of the phonemic contrasts, morphological endings, and major sentence patterns; and (2) were not old enough to be influenced by the formal school situation and the written language. Our search for suitable subjects was at times discouraging, particularly since we tried to control certain variables like IQ, verbal ability, absence of speech defects, and socioeconomic and educational background. We also attempted to find subjects with no previous knowledge of Spanish whose parents were motivated to have their children exposed maximally to the new language and culture during their stay in Madrid. All subjects arrived in Spain at approximately the same time, with no previous knowledge of Spanish. Through the regular use of questionnaires accompanying each recording session, it was estimated that each child spent approximately 20 to 25 hours per week communicating in Spanish, and as much as 30 to 35 additional hours listening to the language, with varying degrees of interest and comprehension.

We had learned from our first year's experience that unsupervised play inside or outside the home was not very productive for recording speech, so all recordings of the six-year olds were made either with peers in supervised play situations inside the home, or with a Spanish-speaking interlocutor conducting a structured interview. In all recording sessions, the principal investigator or the research associate took careful written notes on the verbal and non-verbal aspects of the situation. Over a ten-month period 20 to 24 recordings were made of each child, averaging about one every two weeks for approximately thirty minutes each, to give us a total of about ten hours for each child.

Transcriptions were made of the recordings with the help of the assistant who interviewed the subject. These transcriptions, together with our notes, helped considerably in the understanding of the utterances produced by the subject and by all other participants in the recording session. The transcriptions were then checked with the recordings and refined by the principal investigator. Although our primary concern was with syntactic structures, some attention was given to phonemic development. Transcriptions were generally made in conventional orthography, except where mispronounced utterances could be described only by phonetic notation.

LINGUISTIC MODEL

In devising an appropriate model for children's second-language learning, our principal aim has been descriptive and generative capability. At the present time when so little evidence is available, we have concentrated on the description of the actual process by which certain children have learned Spanish. Ultimately, we hope to develop what might be called a psycholinguistic grammar which would predict the order in which certain linguistic structures and functions are learned.

Using our psycholinguistic model, we shall explore evidence for the existence of universals by analyzing the order of occurrence of specific structures observed among the subjects in our study. Instead of attempting too broad a grammatical coverage, we shall limit ourselves to certain aspects of a single constituent, the verb phrase (VP), and deal specifically with that component referred to as the auxiliary (AUX). We recognize the difficulties in constructing a sub-grammar because the formulation of one rule will invariably affect others in the grammar. Nevertheless, we shall arbitrarily restrict our discussion here to components of the VP for the purpose of making a meaningful comparison.

In developing a linguistic model for the Spanish VP we have been guided by Chomsky (1965), Stevens (1966), Jacobs and Rosenbaum (1968), and Falk (1968), which we interpret as follows:

$$VP \rightarrow AUX \left\{ COP \left\{ \begin{matrix} PRED \\ ADV \\ S' \end{matrix} \right\} \\ VERB\ (S')\ (NP) \right\} (ADV)$$

According to this rule, every utterance containing a VP in Spanish must have the component AUX, regardless of whether the copula or another verb is used. Even if the final derived surface sentence does not actually show some form of AUX, there is in the deep structure at least some representation of this component.

The elements comprising AUX may be shown as follows:

$$\overset{1}{AUX} \rightarrow \overset{}{T}\ \overset{2}{(ha\text{-}+\text{-}do)}\ \overset{3}{(está+\text{-}ndo)}\ \overset{4}{(\text{-}haber)}$$

$$T \rightarrow \left\{ \begin{matrix} present \\ preterite \\ imperfect \end{matrix} \right\} \left\{ \begin{matrix} I \\ II \\ III \\ IV \\ V \\ VI \end{matrix} \right\}$$

(1) T represents an obligatory marker for tense and person number;[1]

---

[1] In order to make our notation more economical, hereafter we may eliminate the need to state both the person and number features under AUX, and simply use person numbers I through VI. Thus persons I, II and III correspond to singular verbs and IV, V and VI correspond to plural forms like *miramos*, *miráis* and *miran*.

(2) the optional element (ha- + -do) expresses relevant anteriority;

(3) (está- + -ndo) stands for explicit duration; and

(4) (-haber) represents subsequence when attached to the V.

Even utterances consisting of only a single form like *mira* 'look' or *ven* 'come' possess the marker T for present tense and second person singular. We may illustrate our formula with various combinations of the present tense form (1) and the three optional modifications (2, 3, 4):

1 + 2	ha mirado
1 + 3	está mirando
1 + 4	mirará
1 + 2 + 3	ha estado mirando
1 + 2 + 4	habrá mirado
1 + 3 + 4	estará mirando
1 + 2 + 3 + 4	habrá estado mirando.

Thus the three elements of relevant anteriority, explicit duration, and subsequence serve as optional modifications of the obligatory tense/person-number element. AUX therefore may be considered an underlying representation bearing in many cases an abstract and indirect relation to the surface structure of even the simplest utterance. This is especially appropriate in describing the process of language learning.

One of the most insightful observations that can be made in language acquisition is to relate children's actual utterances to the intermediate structures generated as a result of applying certain base and transformation rules as described in generative grammar. Thus an utterance like:

*yo quiere voy de mi clase: 'I want I go out of my class'

may be considered an intermediate step between the deep structure represented as two sentences, one embedded in the VP of the other:

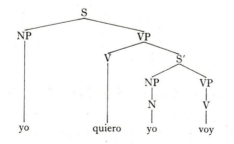

and the surface structure:

yo quiero ir: 'I want to go'.

Within this theoretical framework we can test our hypothesis that second-language learning may involve certain universals by comparing the sequence of structures observed in the output of several children. Support for our hypothesis would be found in any significant similarity among subjects in the ordering of these structures.

Our discussion for the remainder of this presentation will be on the development of the component AUX in our most productive subject, Michael, which will allow us to compare the order of structures observed in his output with that of three other subjects.

DEVELOPMENT OF AUX IN MICHAEL'S SPANISH

The earliest verb forms appearing in Michael's Spanish are imperatives in the singular such as:

> *Mira!:* 'Look!'
> *Francisco, ven:* 'Francisco, come'.

Similar to the constituents Question (Q) and Negative (NEG), the Imperative (IMP) will be considered an optional constituent in the base:

$$S \rightarrow (PRE) \ (NEG) \ NP \ VP$$
$$PRE \rightarrow \left\{ \begin{matrix} Q \\ IMP \end{matrix} \right\}$$

Therefore, in a sentence like *Francisco, ven* we would have the following deep structure:

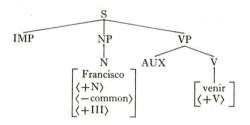

The IMP would then set off a series of transformations by which:

(1) $\langle +IMP \rangle$ would be added as a feature of AUX;
(2) the person feature $\langle +II \rangle$ would be inserted in the AUX;
(3) the number feature of the NP would be copied on the AUX;
(4) any person features in the NP would be deleted;

giving us an intermediate structure like:

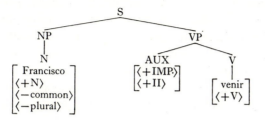

Later transformations at the morphophonemic level would incorporate the features of AUX into V and turn out the appropriate form '*ven*'.

With the occurrence of the copula verb (COP) in recording no. 3, as in

este es: 'this is'.

AUX would assume the features $\langle +\text{COP}\rangle$, $\langle +\text{present}\rangle$, and $\langle +\text{III}\rangle$. An utterance like *está por aquí* 'it's over here' simply represents an expansion of the COP, indicating that another word may now be selected from the child's lexicon to fill that slot.

The first appearances of verbs other than imperative and copula forms are made in recording no. 6, when we find:

tienes aquí: 'you have (it) here'.

At this time we find:

no lo tieno: 'I don't have it'.

We now assign the following features to AUX:

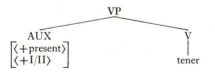

Also appearing now is:

no hay televisión: 'there's no television'.

In recording no. 8, we find the first occurrences of *ir a* plus infinitive, as in:

voy a bajar: 'I'm going downstairs'

and of the present perfect form in utterences like:

Gina ha roto un castillo: 'Gina has broken a castle'
Mira has hecho aquí (for: *Mira lo que has hecho aquí*): 'Look at what you have done here'.

To represent the present perfect form of the verb in the deep structure, we use the present tense plus the modification showing relevant anteriority, ⟨+ha-+-do⟩, which corresponds in the surface structure to the appropriate form of *haber* 'to have' plus *-do*, the suffix added to verbs to form the past participle. Thus *termina-* plus *-do* with the necessary shift in stress gives us *terminado*, which, when preceded by the form of *haber* corresponding to the pronoun *tú*, gives us *has terminado*. In generating irregular forms like *hecho* 'made' and *roto* 'broken', we use transformation rules and the appropriate selection from the lexicon to derive *ha roto* and *has hecho*. The deep structure of AUX now possesses the features:

$$
\text{AUX} \\
\begin{bmatrix} \langle + \text{I/II/III} \rangle \\ \langle + \text{ha-}+\text{-do} \rangle \end{bmatrix}
$$

At this point we find the hortatory as in:

vamos a dibujar: 'let's draw'.

In recording no. 9 we have the verb plus infinitive construction:

quiero pintar: 'I want to paint'.

The next new verb tense to appear is the preterite occurring in recordings 9 and 11 in sentences like:

no sé qué dijo esto: 'I don't know what this one said'
se cayó el dragón: 'the dragon fell down'.

In the AUX we now include the tense feature ⟨+preterite⟩.

We cannot assume at this point that the child possesses the competence to use the preterite form in all three persons, singular and plural. It would be more accurate to combine the new feature ⟨+preterite⟩ with the feature ⟨+III⟩, giving ⟨+III preterite⟩. Furthermore, this combination is applicable only to those verbs that the child can produce at this time in the third person singular form of the preterite tense. Such a detailed description would be feasible with a computer. For the purpose of our discussion here, we choose to simplify our description to demonstrate our method of comparison.

At approximately the same time, in recording no. 11, we observe the use of the progressive form:

El señor está mirando: 'The man is watching.'

Like ⟨+ha-+-do⟩, we assign the feature ⟨+está-+-ndo⟩ to the

base as an underlying abstraction relating to the progressive form *está mirando* in the surface structure.

We now observe these utterances:

> *son malos:* 'they are bad'
> *se caen:* 'they fall down'.

We may add the feature ⟨+VI⟩ to AUX. Michael now gives evidence of distinguishing the plural from the singular, since he has also used acceptably the constructions *es malo* 'it is bad' and *se cae* 'he falls down'.

In recordings 13 and 14 more preterite forms appear, now extending the child's competence to include the combination of features ⟨+IV⟩ and ⟨+preterite⟩:

> *ya que vinimos aquí en la noche* (for: *ya que venimos...*): 'since we came here during the night.'

During this same period, we observe the use of more tenses, as in the following utterances:

> *cuando éramos en colegio otra vez:* 'when we were in school again'
> *era bonito:* 'it was pretty'

demonstrating the tense feature ⟨+imperfect⟩ which is assigned to AUX. At this point we may observe that the child now has all three tense features: ⟨+present⟩, ⟨+preterite⟩, and ⟨+imperfect⟩.

Also at this period in the child's learning of Spanish we note the use of the expression *tener que* followed by an infinitive:

> *tiene que scribir mi* (for: *tienes que escribir para mí*) (or perhaps for: *...dibujarme*): 'you have to write (this for) me' ('you have to draw me')

In recordings 14–22, we can observe the use of the subjunctive in the following utterances:

> *¡Que no tires!:* 'Don't throw (it)!'
> *¿Quieres que tire otro...?:* 'Do you want me to throw another one...?'
> *Después cuando se caiga...:* 'Afterwards when he falls...'
> *Voy a decir a mi mamá que lo doble:* 'I'm going to tell my mother to fold it.'

In recording 22 the past progressive construction can be seen with the use of the imperfect tense plus ⟨+está-+-ndo⟩, as in the following utterances:

> *cuando estábamos subiendo las escaleras:* 'when we were climbing the stairs'
> *no estabas buscando éste:* 'you weren't looking for this'.

This tense may be stated in terms of the following features:

AUX
$$\begin{bmatrix} \langle+\text{II/IV}\rangle \\ \langle+\text{imperfect}\rangle \\ \langle+\text{está-}+\text{-ndo}\rangle \end{bmatrix}$$

In recordings 28–30 we observe the first combinations of the features ⟨+present⟩ and ⟨+-haber⟩ expressing both probability, as in:

> *será un amigo de los* (for: ...*de ellos*)*:* 'he must be a friend of theirs'

and subsequence, as in:

> *te lo enseñaré:* 'I'll show it to you'
> *aquí lo pondré:* 'I'll put it here'
> *yo te lo explicaré:* 'I'll explain it to you'.

In recording 38, the child distinguishes between affirmative and negative commands:

> *hazlo:* 'do it'
> *no hagas:* 'don't do (it)'

adding to AUX the combination of features:

AUX
$$\begin{bmatrix} \langle+\text{IMP}\rangle \\ \langle+\text{NEG}\rangle \end{bmatrix}$$

which now contrasts with the existing structure of AUX having either IMP or NEG, but not both.

We find an example of the imperfect subjunctive:

> *si lo tuviera aquí ponía* (for: *pondría*)*:* 'if I had it I would put a soldier here'.

It is questionable, however, whether or not to attribute this feature to the child's competence at this time since he gives evidence later on in recordings 31 through 39 of still not being able to control the past subjunctive. Instead he uses the imperfect tense:

> *y después no quería que bajaba* (for: ...*bajara*)*:* 'and then he didn't want me to go downstairs'.

This raises the problem relating to all studies on language acquisition: When can we assume that the child has learned a particular structure? It is clear that the learning of a particular structure does not just happen abruptly but takes place over a period of time. In one particular example, Michael reaches a point when he expresses awareness of a specific grammatical concept. In the utterance

> *Yo pinta...yo pinte...pinto un avión:* 'I paint...I paint...I paint an airplane'

he searches for the appropriate verb inflection, and finally succeeds in applying the rule satisfactorily. Only minutes later, however, in the same recording and in subsequent recordings, the child again produces:

> *yo pinta un avión*

with the inappropriate verb ending.

One possible approach to the question of when a particular grammatical structure is actually learned is to apply a measure of frequency. Of the total output of a child's utterances containing a certain type of construction, a significant percentage of acceptable constructions would indicate that the learner has this particular grammatical concept under control. Once again, however, this type of analysis would be more appropriate with the aid of an electronic computer.

In recordings 40 through 49, the last samplings taken of Michael's learning of Spanish, we find different person-number forms indicating greater control of concepts which had appeared earlier. There is vacillation in the use of the subjunctive in constructions with *antes que* and *cuando:*

> *él va a venir cuando nos vamos a casa* (for: *...vayamos a casa*): 'he's going to come when we go home'
> *pero antes que me voy en la guerra* (for: *me vaya a la guerra*): 'but before I go to war'
> *cuando sea mayor:* 'when I am bigger'.

There are more occurrences of the imperfect tense, used this time in place of the conditional, as in polite requests:

> *¿me podía dar un calamelo?* (for: *¿me podría dar un caramelo?*): 'could you give me a piece of candy?'

Here we may ask whether *podía* or *podría* constitutes acceptable speech on the part of the child, since many native speakers of standard Spanish substitute the imperfect form for the conditional. We must rule out any phonological error, since Michael is past the stage where the cluster /-dr-/ causes any difficulty. In any event we do not credit the child with the competence to use this construction.

At this point we shall summarize the various verb features discussed in this presentation, and by assigning a symbol to each structure as found in Michael's output, we may then compare the order of learning of similar structures in our other subjects. In Table 1 the first column shows the structures in Michael's Spanish according to the recording in which they were first observed. The other columns represent the structures observed in other subjects which are marked with symbols based on Michael's sequence of structures. While the actual number of the recording is useful in giving us an overall perspective of the learning process, it is less meaningful than the sequence of specific structures as they are observed in the data.

In all four subjects included in our comparison, we find the earliest forms appearing to be the imperative and the copula, followed closely by other verbs in the present indicative. Next in order after the first appearances of the present indicative, we observe in three out of four children the use of the preterite tense and the present perfect, followed by the present progressive construction. Of all tenses observed, the future shows up last or nearly last in three of the children, and in all four children, the conditional does not appear at all. Michael, whose sampling over a two-year period was more than twice that of the other children, is the only child showing the use of the past subjunctive. In all subjects we find the singular forms occurring first, with VI as the first plural form to appear. In three out of four subjects we find IV as the last to appear in our data, while the other subject included in this comparison did not show evidence of learning IV at all. In all subjects there is a lack of evidence for the use of person V, corresponding to forms such as *cantáis* and *tenéis*.

Since three out of four subjects show III occurring earliest, we hypothesize that the order of learning takes place something like the following: a child first learns III as in *pinta* or *dispara*, resembling the imperative, a form that is apparently learned early by all our subjects. It is likely that an imperative like *¡mira!* or *¡dispara!* easily leads to the formation of an utterance with the III person since the only requirement structurally is a change in intonation. Thus, *¡Dispara una bala!* 'Shoot a

TABLE I. *Order of appearance of verb phrase elements*

Recording no.	Michael	O	Mcy	S
1	1a, 1b	1a–b, 2a–d	2a–e, 4, 6a	1a, 2d–e, 4
2	—	4	7b	1b, 2a–c
3	2a–e	—	—	—
4	3	—	1a, 3, 6b, 8	—
5	—	5a	5a	5a, 5c, 7b
6	4	—	1b	5b
7	—	7b	—	—
8	5a, 5b, 5c	6a, 7a	5b	—
9	6a, 6b	9	—	—
10	—	2e	—	—
11	7a, 7b, 7c	3, 5b	—	7c
12	—	—	9, 7a, 13	—
13	8	7c, 8, 11	—	—
14	9	—	—	—
15	—	—	—	—
16	—	—	—	6b, 7a
17	—	6b	—	11
18	—	—	10	6a, 13
19	—	5c	—	—
⋮				
22	10	—	—	—
⋮				
29	11	—	—	—
⋮				
35	12	—	—	—
⋮				
38	13	—	—	—

Key for verb phrase elements[1]

1a	Imperative	6a	Verb + infinitive
1b	Imperative expanded	6b	Preterite
2a	COP *es*	7a	< + está- + -ndo > present progressive
2b	COP *está*	7b	VI
2c	III	7c	IV
2d	Present indicative (non-COP verb)	8	Imperfect
2e	II	9	Present subjunctive
3	*hay*	10	Past progressive
4	I	11	Future
5a	*ir a* + infinitive	12	Present subjunctive
5b	< + ha- + -do > present perfect	13	Negative imperative
5c	Hortatory		

[1] Elements are numbered according to order of appearance, with different letters for those constructions occurring simultaneously.

DANIEL P. DATO

bullet!', meaning perhaps, 'You, Francisco, shoot a bullet!', easily leads to *¡Dispara una bala!*, with the meaning 'He shoots a bullet.'

The II then appears, with the addition of final *-s* as in *Tú disparas a éste* 'You're shooting at this one', followed by I as in *yo disparo* 'I shoot', which at first may alternate with the inappropriate inflection *-a* as in **yo dispara* or **yo pinta*. With the verb *tener*, Michael shows the sequence: *tiene, tienes* and then **tieno* which is later replaced by the standard form *tengo*. Person VI appears when the child simply adds the final *-n* as in verbs like *tienen, están* and *juegan*.

TABLE 2. *Chart showing sequence of person-number marker*

Michael	O	Mcy	S
III	III	I, II, III	I, II
II	I	—	III
I	II	—	—
VI	VI	VI	VI
IV	IV	—	IV

Person IV appears last in our data, occurring in forms like *podemos*, *tenemos* and *estamos;* and V, corresponding to the inflection in the forms *estáis, tenéis* and *cantáis*, do not appear at all in our sampling.

CONCLUSION

We interpret as significant the similarities in the order of occurrence of certain underlying structures and functions in the subjects studied. The sequences of person-number, tense and other elements of the auxiliary are similar enough to suggest the existence of systematic patterning in the learning of Spanish as a second language by English-speaking children. By comparing the output of Michael, who started learning Spanish at age four years and one month, with that of the other subjects, ages five years and six months to six years and three months, it is suggested that this difference in age may be of little or no consequence in second-language learning. Undoubtedly there is a need for more studies of second-language learning in the natural foreign environment. Furthermore, by comparing findings on the learning of Spanish as a second language with the acquisition of Spanish as a native language, we are confident that this avenue of research will contribute greatly to our understanding of language learning in general.

32

BIBLIOGRAPHY

Chomsky, Noam. *Aspects of the theory of syntax*. Cambridge, Mass.: M.I.T. Press, 1965.

Dato, Daniel P. *Children's acquisition of Spanish syntax in the foreign environment*. Mimeo, 1969.

Falk, Julia S. *Nominalizations in Spanish*. Studies in Linguistics and Language Learning, vol. 5. Seattle: University of Washington Press, 1968.

Jacobs, Roderick A., and Rosenbaum, Peter S. *English Transformational grammar*. Waltham, Mass.: Blaisdell Publishing Company, 1968.

Stevens, Claire E. *A characterization of Spanish nouns and adjectives*. Studies in Linguistics and Language Learning, vol. 2. Seattle: University of Washington Press, 1966.

4 *The psychologically relevant data of second-language learning*

LARRY SELINKER

It may not be unfair to say that, as we approach this conference, many of us feel that a sense of malaise has set into the field of applied linguistics. Nowhere is this more evident than in the area which attempts to relate psycholinguistics to second-language learning. I would guess that most of us know that after a decade of research, a realistic theoretical framework does not exist and conflicting opinions and imprecise hypotheses still abound. It seems to me that the worst feature of this stage in the development of our field, is our inability to unambiguously identify the phenomena we wish to study. This paper is based on the belief that particularly in this area, rapid progress can be made.[1]

Consider the title of this paper. The 'psychologically relevant data of second-language learning' should be those data which when elicited and described in certain specific ways will lead to an understanding of the structures and processes underlying attempted meaningful performance in a second language. Unfortunately, how to get these data is not immediately obvious to the analyst. We hypothesize here that the class of behavioral events which are to count as relevant in a theory of second-language learning has to be organized with the aid of theoretical constructs of the sort I will sketch in this paper.

If in a psychology of second-language learning our goal is explanation of some important aspects of the latent psychological structures of an individual whenever he attempts to perceive second-language events or produce a second-language norm, then it seems to me that we are

---

[1] This paper was written during 1969, while I was a visiting Fulbright lecturer at the Department of Applied Linguistics, University of Edinburgh. Many students and staff members, through their persistent calls for clarity, have helped me to crystallize background ideas, as well as much of the content presented herein; I especially wish to thank my colleague Ruth Clark for her insight and patience.

concerned in large part with what Weinreich (1953, pp. 7–8) has called 'interlingual identifications'. In his book *Languages in contact*, Weinreich discusses – albeit briefly – the practical need for assuming in a bilingual study that identifications such as phoneme /p/ in two languages or a grammatical relationship in two languages have been equated by an individual in a language contact situation. Weinreich tackles many relevant linguistic questions and some psychological ones, but leaves open questions regarding the psychological structure of what I have chosen to call the 'domain of interlingual identifications'. Weinreich thus has no responsibility for the idealized structure of this domain, which I shall attempt to sketch in the remainder of this talk.

The learner of a second language from the beginning of his study has his attention riveted upon some aspect of a norm of the second language whose utterances he is attempting to understand and produce, whose texts he is trying to read, and so on. In line with generally accepted usage, let us call this second language the 'target language' (TL). In other words, from the beginning of his study of a second language, the learner has his attention riveted upon the norm of the TL whose utterances he is attempting to produce. Notice that we have simplified our idealized picture, first of all, by assuming that whether it be prescriptive, descriptive, or a combination of the two, there is only *one* norm of only *one* TL within the interlingual focus of attention of our idealized second-language learner. Note further that in this picture, there are no individual differences, a most unrealistic constraint but one that I cannot deal with here and will have to leave until another occasion.[1]

We have also simplified our idealized description of the domain of interlingual identifications by focusing our analytical attention upon the only observable meaningful data we have, i.e. the utterances which are produced as a result of the learner's attempted production of a TL norm. This set of utterances for *most* learners of a second language is not identical to the hypothesized corresponding set of utterances which would have been produced by a native speaker of the TL had he attempted to express the same meaning as the learner.[2] Since we can

[1] See Lawler and Selinker (in press) for an attempt to handle this tricky question in terms of profiles of idealized learners who differ one from the other with respect to types of linguistic rules and types of meaningful performance in a second language.
[2] Clearly, the interlanguage performance of *some* second-language learners is not distinguishable from performance in the TL by native speakers of that TL. Since individuals who achieve what we might, in this case, legitimately call

observe that these two sets of utterances are not identical, then researchers in the psychology of second-language learning are completely
justified, in fact I would say *compelled*, to hypothesize a separate linguistic system based on the observable output which results from a
learner's attempted production of a TL norm.

Thus, within the domain of interlingual identifications any learner of
a second language has (1) knowledge underlying production in his
native language (NL); (2) knowledge – presumably at more than one
level of consciousness – about the TL; and (3) knowledge underlying
attempted production of a TL norm.[1] In an experimental paper concerning language transfer (Selinker, 1969), I have chosen to call the
result of this attempted production of a TL norm 'interlanguage' (IL).
It is obvious that the only observable meaningful data we as analysts
have which are directly related to these three types of knowledge are
(1) NL utterances, (2) IL utterances, and (3) TL utterances, the latter
as produced by native speakers of that TL. These three sets of utterances then are the relevant data of a theory of second-language learning,
and I would argue that theoretical predictions in such a theory should be
primarily concerned with the surface structures of sentences related to
IL utterances.

By setting up these three linguistic systems under one umbrella, as it
were, and by gathering data relevant to specific linguistic structures in
three systems under the *same* experimental conditions, the investigator
in the psychology of second-language learning can begin to study what
he should be studying: the processes which establish the knowledge which
in turn underlies IL behaviour. I would like to suggest that these
processes are at least five-fold: first, 'language transfer'; secondly,
'transfer-of-training'; thirdly, 'strategies of learning'; fourthly,
strategies of communication'; and fifthly, 'overgeneralization of linguistic material'. Each of the analyst's predictions as to the surface
structures of IL sentences should be made relative to one or more of
these processes.

Before briefly describing these processes, another notion I wish to
introduce for your consideration is the concept of 'fossilization'.
Fossilizable structures are linguistic phenomena which speakers of a
language will tend to keep in their IL relative to another language, no

'native speaker competence' are relatively few and far between, I think we
should ignore them for now and can safely do so.
[1] 'Transitional competence' in Corder's terms (Corder, 1967).

37

matter what the age of the learner or the amount of instruction he receives in the TL. I have in mind fossilizable structures such as the well known 'errors': French uvular /r/ in the IL of French speakers relative to English, American English retroflex /r/ in the IL of these speakers relative to French, English rhythm in the IL relative to Spanish, German *Time-Place* order after the verb in the IL of German speakers relative to English, and so on. I also have in mind less well known 'non-errors', such as Spanish monophthong vowels in the IL of Spanish speakers relative to Hebrew and Hebrew *Object-Time* order after the verb in the IL of Hebrew speakers relative to English. Finally, there are fossilizable structures that are much harder to classify, such as some features of the Thai tone system in the IL of Thai speakers relative to English. These fossilizable structures tend to remain as potential performance, reemerging in the productive performance of the IL even when seemingly eradicated. Many of these phenomena reappear in IL performance when the speaker's attention is focused on new and seemingly difficult subject matter and/or when he appears to be in an anxiety state. This reappearance is not solely limited to the phonetic level. For example, some of the subtlest information that a learner of a second language has to master regards subcategorization notions of verbal complementation. Indian English as an IL with regard to English seems to fossilize the *V that* construction for all verbs that take sentential complements.[1] Even when the correct form has been learned by the Indian speaker of English, this type of information is the first he seems to lose when his attention is diverted to new intellectual subject matter and/or when he has not spoken the TL for even a short time.

It is my contention that the most interesting phenomena in IL performance are those items, rules, and subsystems which are fossilizable, and that investigators should concentrate on them, trying to relate them to the five processes listed above.[2] If it can be experimentally

[1] Keith Brown has argued (personal communication) that the sociolinguistic status of the 'languages' or 'dialects' called Indian English, Filipino English, West African English, West African French, and so on, places them in a different category from that of the IL situation which I have been describing. From the sociolinguistic point of view this argument might be justified, but I am concerned in this paper with a psychological perspective and the relevant idealizations seem to me to be identical in all of these cases.

[2] This paragraph is quoted in its entirety in Jakobovits (1970, p. 87); the quote there, however, is from an earlier draft of this paper. The only substantive change between the two versions is the labeling of the fifth process which is there called: 'reorganization of linguistic material'. Paul Van Buren has rightly

demonstrated that fossilizable items, rules, and subsystems which occur in IL performance are a result of the NL, then we are dealing with the process of 'language transfer'; if these fossilizable items, rules, and subsystems are a result of identifiable items in training procedures, then we are dealing with the process known as the 'transfer-of-training'; if they are a result of an identifiable approach by the learner to the material to be learned, then we are dealing with 'strategies of learning'; if they are a result of an identifiable approach by the learner to communicating with native speakers of the TL, then we are dealing with 'strategies of communication'; and, finally, if they are a result of a clear overgeneralization of TL rules and semantic features, then we are dealing with the 'overgeneralization of linguistic material'. I would like to hypothesize that these five processes are *processes* which are *central* to second-language learning, and that each process forces fossilizable material upon surface IL utterances, controlling to a very large extent the shape of these utterances.[1]

If researchers in the psychology of second-language learning were to follow my suggestions and begin looking for, describing, and experimentally validating fossilizable items, rules, and subsystems in interlanguages, and relating these to the above-mentioned processes, where would all this activity lead them? I cannot, of course, predict. What I find most promising for study is the claim that many IL tendencies are *never* really eradicated for most second-language learners but are still somehow psychologically there, and regularly reappear for these

called the following to my attention: first, this process does not seem to involve any actual 'reorganization'; secondly, the title of the process in the earlier draft is very confusing since the notion of 'reorganization' is central to the definition of 'learning' a second language, hinted at in the earlier draft and made more explicit later on in this version. I apologize to the reader for this confusion.

[1] Coulter in his thesis (1968) presents convincing data to demonstrate entirely fossilizable IL competences, which seem to be due not only to language transfer but also to a strategy of communication common to many learners which dictates to them, internally as it were, that they know enough of the TL in order to communicate. And they stop learning. Whether they stop learning entirely or go on to learn in a minor way, e.g. adding vocabulary as Mahavir Jain insists they must, is it seems to me, a moot point. If these individuals do not also learn the syntactic information that goes with lexical items, then adding a few new lexical items, say on space travel, is, I would argue, of little consequence. But the important thing is that fossilization of entire IL competences is a widespread occurrence with Indian English (Jain, 1969).

learners under conditions of anxiety and shifting attention, and performance in new skills.

There are certainly many questions one may wish to ask regarding these notions; I shall deal with four. First, can we always unambiguously identify which of these five processes our observable data are to be attributable to? Most probably not. Sometimes, for example, we may not know whether a particular constituent IL concatenation is a result of language transfer or the transfer-of-training or, perhaps, of both. But this limitation need not deter us. We have an enormous amount of unambiguous data lying before us when these data are arranged as suggested here.

Another problem concerns the apparent impossibility of fitting the following type of question into the idealized domain I have been sketching: how does a second-language-learning novice become able to produce IL utterances whose constituents are in the correct order, i.e. 'correct' with respect to the TL whose norm he is attempting to produce? It seems to me that this question, though relevant to the psychology of second-language learning, is one that should not be asked at the present time since its asking depends upon our understanding clearly the psychological limits and extent of interlingual identifications. That is, before we can discover how surface constituents that are in an IL get reorganized from that IL to identity with the TL, we must have a clear idea of what is in that IL. In the experiments on language transfer referred to previously I would claim to have shown that within a very limited interlingual situation, the basis from which linguistic material must be *reorganized* in order to be 'correct', has been operationally and unambiguously established, but I have there said nothing about how successful learners do in fact reorganize from this particular IL. Here we can speculate that 'learning' a second language, to a large extent, involves reorganizing linguistic material from an IL to a particular TL.

The third problem is: what are the relevant units of this hypothesized domain of interlingual identifications and is there any evidence for their existence? If the relevant data of the psychology of second-language learning are in fact parallel utterances in three productive linguistic systems (NL, IL, and TL), then it seems to me reasonable to hypothesize that the only relevant, one might say 'psychologically real', interlingual unit is one which can simultaneously be described for experimentally induced parallel data in the three systems. I have nothing experimentally relevant to say about underlying and realizational structure, but for evidence of the relevant unit of surface syntactic structure, applying at one and the same time to these three linguistic systems, I refer you once again to experimental evidence appearing in my paper on language transfer: the interlingual unit of surface structure in these experiments was labelled the 'syntactic string', a unit roughly equivalent to the traditional direct object or to an adverb of place, or adverb of time, adverb of manner, and so on. I would claim that the syntactic string has a behavioral unity, both in and out of the experimental situation, which accounts for a large class of IL events.

Concerning the notion of relevant units on the phonological level, it seems to me that Brière (1968) has demonstrated that for his data there are several relevant units:[1] the relevant units do not necessarily correspond to linguistic units, but rather would depend on the sounds involved. If I may be allowed to 'reinterpret' his data, it seems to me that he has explicitly been working with three and only three systems: first, NL utterances which were hypothesized utterances in American English: secondly, TL utterances which were actual utterances in the 'composite' language he set up, each utterance having been produced by a native speaker of French, Arabic, and Vietnamese; and thirdly, IL utterances which were actual utterances produced by native speakers of this NL when attempting to produce this particular TL norm. Regarding the sounds /ž/ and /ŋ/ in his corpus, the unit stretching across these three systems is the taxonomic phoneme defined distributionally within the syllable as opposed to within the word (p. 73). For other sounds the relevant phonological unit of interlingual identifications is *not* this taxonomic phoneme, but would be based on phonetic parameters, some of which he claims are probably not known (p. 64).

If these units which appear in the domain of interlingual identifications are not the same units as those in the native-speaker domain, then where in fact do they come from? An interesting bit of speculation about native speaker performance units is provided by Haggard (1967, p. 335) who

---

[1] Though Brière has not presented his subjects with stimuli that are meaningful to them, I find his experiments very 'meaningful' in the sense that there is no superimposition of outside models upon his data. Furthermore, Brière's experimental procedure is quite relevant in that it imitated to a large extent methods of language teaching proposed by structural linguists. He hints (p. 74) that it may be impossible to extend psychological learning theory to cover data such as his, and that the classes and subclasses of structural linguistic theory are not sufficient to predict difficulty in learning second-language phonology.

states that searching for 'the unit' in native-speaker speech-perception is a waste of time. Alternative units may be available to native speakers, for example under noise conditions.[1] If it is at all reasonable to postulate alternative linguistic units available to individuals under different conditions, then it seems to me reasonable for us to postulate a type of unit that stretches across three linguistic systems: NL, IL, and TL. This interlingual unit becomes available to an individual whenever he attempts to produce a TL norm, becoming available only when he switches his psychic state from the native-speaker domain into the new domain of interlingual identifications. I would like to postulate further that these relevant units of interlingual identifications do not come from anywhere; they are latent in the brain, available to an individual whenever he wishes to attempt to produce the norm of a TL.

Finally, how can we experiment with three linguistic systems, creating the same experimental conditions for each, with one unit stretching across these systems? I can only refer you once again to my own experiments on language transfer (Selinker, 1969), where desired concatenations of particular surface syntactic structures were obtained in what I would claim was an efficient and valid manner. An oral interview technique was used; the purpose of that interview was to achieve a similar framework in the three systems which served the interviewer as a guide in his attempt to elicit certain types of sentences from the subjects. Upon request, I am prepared to make available a transcript of this interview as well as some thoughts for its improvement. Future experimental work ought to go toward investigating the kind and extent of linguistic structures amenable to this particular technique.

BIBLIOGRAPHY

Brière, Eugène J. *A psycholinguistic study of phonological interference.* The Hague: Mouton, 1968.
Corder, S. P. 'The significance of the learner's errors.' *IRAL*, 5 (1967), 161–70.
Coulter, Kenneth. 'Linguistic error-analysis of the spoken English of two native Russians.' Thesis, University of Washington, 1968.
Haggard, Mark P. 'Models and data in speech perception.' In Wathen-Dunn, 1967.
Jain, Mahavir. 'Error analysis of an Indian English corpus.' Unpublished paper, University of Edinburgh, 1969.

[1] The fact that Haggard is concerned with alternate units which are inclusive in larger units has no bearing on the issue under discussion here. His bit of speculation that is relevant here concerns the intriguing possibility of alternate language units being available to individuals.

Jakobovits, Leon A. *Foreign language learning: a psycholinguistic analysis of the issues*. Rowley, Mass.: Newbury House, 1970.

Lawler, John, and Selinker, Larry. 'On paradoxes, rules, and research in second language learning.' *Language Learning* (in press).

Selinker, Larry. 'Language transfer.' *General Linguistics*, 9 (1969), 67–92.

Wathen-Dunn, Weiant (ed.). *Models for the perception of speech and visual form*. Cambridge, Mass.: M.I.T. Press, 1967.

Weinreich, Uriel. *Languages in contact*. The Hague: Mouton, 1968. (Originally published as no. 1 in the series 'Publications of the Linguistic Circle of New York,' 1953.)

5   Inferencing: a process in using and learning language

AARON S. CARTON

Inferencing is a coined term.[1] It is intended to refer to a process of identifying unfamiliar stimuli. In foreign language learning inferencing is concerned with the acquisition of new morphemes and vocables in 'natural' contexts.

The term may be allowed to suggest, but not denote, *unconscious inference* which is the English translation of the German expression *unbewusster Schluss* by which Wundt, Helmholtz and other early psychologists designated the very rapid, irresistible, unconscious integration of sensed attributes.[2] But inferencing should not be allowed to become synonomous with *unbewusster Schluss* because that term was used to designate the apprehension of known or familiar objects that are available as concepts because of earlier experience. In inferencing, attributes and contexts that are familiar are utilized in recognizing what is *not* familiar. Inferencing probably proceeds more slowly than the *unbewusster Schluss*.

Inferencing may suggest, but not denote, the formal logical inference used in science or law, which is the method of drawing permissible conclusions from available data. But inferencing should not be allowed to become synonomous with logical inference. To be sure, inferencing is concerned with the implications of convergent cues, but it does not demand that high levels of rigor and formality be adhered to. The inferencing language learner accepts levels of probability and uncertainty that are not likely to be permitted in making acceptable formal inferences.

---

[1] The research reported in this paper was conducted pursuant to Contracts OE 4-14-021 and OE 5-14-024 with the United States Office of Education, Department of Health, Education, and Welfare, while the writer was affiliated with New York University and the City University of New York.
[2] Boring (1950).

Inferencing is a much more rapid, haphazard and subjective process than logical inference.

This paper is concerned first with inferencing as a psychological process. An operational definition of the term may, in fact, be suggested by the experiments and illustrations involving inferencing that will be discussed. Next a sketch will be offered of the kinds of analysis of language and language learning situations that are germane to a foreign language pedagogy that would involve inferencing. The conclusion will touch on the educational commitments and kinds of objectives that may be served by inferencing or that are implied by using it. The initial research on inferencing has merely begun to uncover and define the problem. Thus, in general, this is a speculative paper presented in the context of continuing research.

SOME ILLUSTRATIONS OF INFERENCING

'Cloze procedure' is a widely used psycholinguistic research technique in which words are deleted from text and respondents are required to attempt to replace them. Obviously, the respondent finds that the cues in the text which remain available to him enable him to do the task. The cues are sometimes completely linguistic when, for example, the structure of the sentence and the morphemes surrounding the deletion suggest a vocable of a specific form class or even a specific function word. On the other hand, the respondent's familiarity with 'the nature of things' and his comprehension of the available portions of the text may suggest to him one or several vocables that may reasonably be returned to the loci of the deletions. Most frequently both kinds of cues are available to solve those Cloze problems that can be solved.

Over eighty years ago Ebbinghaus used the task of recovering deletions in an effort to ascertain intellectual fatigue at different times in the school day.[1] It failed to function as a measure of fatigue but it did prove to be a rather reliable and valid indicator of the intellectual functioning demanded for school performance.

Wilson Taylor, who coined the term 'Cloze procedure,' attempted to measure the 'readability' of texts by determining the proportions of deletions that could be returned to the texts by panels of readers.[2] In studying the competences of the readers who served on his panels, Taylor discovered that aptness with Cloze procedure was rather highly

[1] Ebbinghaus (1897).   [2] Taylor (1953).

correlated with the conventional measure of intelligence used by the United States Army.[1]

When Carroll, Carton, and Wilds attempted to measure achievement in foreign language study by means of Cloze procedure they found that the procedure could, *only to a degree*, measure achievement in acquiring a foreign language as such achievement was at the time conventionally understood.[2] The test scores of the respondents were found to be heavily confounded by other factors, which might have been designated as 'ability to do Cloze' which appeared obtrusively in both their native and foreign languages. Eventually, Carton found that if he allowed his respondents credit for providing merely a grammatical description for a deleted vocable, he could get results that correlated well with convention- al tests of foreign language achievement.[3]

The results of studies of Cloze procedure suggest a question about the widespread assertion that linguistic competence is a universal human phenomenon that bears no relation to other intellectual functions.[4] Can a distinction be viably and usefully maintained between linguistic com- petence, on one hand, and the role of experience and intellectual func- tioning, on the other hand, when one is concerned with *communication* by means of language and not merely the intuition as to which utterances may be acceptable or grammatical in a language?

The respondent to a Cloze test does not identify a new word. He merely illustrates the fact that context may provide him with cues for identifying a new word. For if a new word were to be inserted where a deletion once stood, the same kinds of cues can be brought to bear in arriving at a *definition* of that word as were brought to bear in selecting a known word that might fit in the deletion. Werner and Kaplan demonstrated this process by means of their Word-Context Test.[5] A typical example of the test required their respondents to define the artificial word *ashder* which was presented in the following six contexts:

1 A lazy man stops working when there is an ashder.
2 An ashder keeps you from doing what you want to do.
3 Mr. Brown said to Mr. Smith; 'I don't think we should start this work because there are ashders.'

[1] Taylor (1957).   [2] Carroll, Carton, and Wilds (1959).
[3] Carton (1959).
[4] See, for example, Chomsky (1968), Lenneberg (in Smith and Miller, 1966), and McNeill (*ibid.*).
[5] Werner and Kaplan (1963).

4 The way is clear if there are no ashders.

5 Before finishing the task he had to get rid of a few ashders.

6 Jan had to turn back because there were ashders in her path.

In arriving at Werner and Kaplan's definition for *ashder* (which is *obstacle*), the reader might note that he merely identified a novel word for a concept that was already available to him. Thus the process that concerned Werner and Kaplan may be regarded as an appropriate (though special) example of inferencing. The fact that the example applies to the acquisition of a novel term – a novel fragment of language – and not to an unfamiliar concept makes it an instance of inferencing.

Similar procedures may, of course, be applied to attaining or forming concepts which were not previously available to the respondent. Some studies, exemplified in the work of Vigotsky,[1] have indeed been concerned with acquiring labels and concepts concurrently. Eventually research in foreign language acquisition may find that is advisable and heuristic to subsume such instances of concept attainment under the rubric of inferencing. Yet this would be inferencing that is combined with other learning processes. It might be said to occur in an example where a child walks up to a cage in a zoo and learns from a sign or from someone's instruction that the term for the creature in the cage is *mongoose*. This kind of learning also retains some of the characteristic risk and probabilism of inferencing in the possibility that the child may conclude that *mongoose* refers to the bars of the cage, the tree within it, or the ants being eaten there, although the desired connection is much more probably established than any other which might have occurred. In any event, the concurrent acquisition of concepts and labels is a rather infrequent occurrence in foreign language acquisition in formal settings. As long as a distinction is established and maintained between the acquisition of labels for available concepts and the acquisition of new concepts, there is little point in detaining oneself at present with determining how each of these processes should be classified.

In Werner and Kaplan's study care was taken lest the novel term to be identified suggest the conventional label for the concept the term was intended to designate. Thus, in the study cited, respondents were to use contexts exclusively. Yet Werner and Kaplan found that young children and schizophrenics exhibited what they called 'homophonic word realism.' That is to say, the appearance of the word was allowed to

[1] Vigotsky (1962).

48

suggest its meaning. Thus the artificial word *corplum,* which was used to designate *stick* in one of their exercises, was interpreted as *corporal* although corplums were described as being long, hard, and useful for walking. Werner and Kaplan thus showed that a distinction is to be retained between cuing from contexts and cuing from the appearance of the novel term.

In acquiring a foreign language that is linguistically related to a language one already knows, there may be frequent cognates, derivatives, and loan words whose appearance (visual or auditory) is suggestive of labels one already knows. The familiar terms frequently turn out to be appropriate translations of the novel terms to be acquired. Thus inferencing, as a process in foreign language acquisition, does not preclude attention to the novel term itself. Such novel terms may provide a special class of cues, to be described below, though we would be well advised to note the possible difficulties attendant upon this class of cues in attempting to teach young children and lunatics to use them.

The fact that the preceding examples do not apply merely to foreign language acquisition might underscore the generality of inferencing as an intellectual process. In addition to the illustrations of inferencing in one's native language cited above, a number of recent studies of the reading process and of reading acquisition have convincingly illustrated the extensive role of contextual and linguistic cues in facilitating learning, comprehension and also in causing occasional mis-readings.[1] (The specifics of these studies need not detain the reader in the present context.) Finally, an experimental analogy of inferencing in the visual domain can, perhaps, illustrate the process in its most general sense.

The Visual Inference Test is a procedure devised to study the range of reactions individuals exhibit to unrecognizable visual stimuli and to the addition of information that might make the stimuli recognizable. In a study using this procedure a photograph of a scene, such as, for example, a table setting, was completely masked by black paper save for a single object (or part of an object) such as a spoon. Spoons were, of course, familiar objects for the respondents but pictures of them are easily rendered unrecognizable by close masking. (The analogy between the visual procedure and inferencing in the linguistic domain is somewhat incomplete at this point because in the visual procedure the stimulus is familiar although its identification is impaired, while in the linguistic procedure a completely novel stimulus is presented.) Once the

---

[1] See, for example, a collection of papers in Goodman and Fleming (1969).

spoon was established as the target to be identified by subjects in the experiment, they were free to guess as to what it might be or they might refuse to do so. They were also asked to indicate how certain they were about their guess. Next an object, such as a cup or a plate, was exposed from elsewhere in the picture. The new information provided the subject with an opportunity to make a second guess about the target object and to indicate his certainty. The procedure was repeated until five cues in addition to the target object were presented. Thus a fork, a knife, a glass and the like all served to suggest to the subject the target object he was to identify. With additional cues the object itself became more recognizable. American secondary school students in foreign language classes served as subjects in the initial studies in which some twenty-five target objects and sets of attendant cues were used. These studies revealed a wide variety of distinctive patterns in respect to frequency, accuracy, and alterations of guesses and in respect to certainty about guesses as the availability of cues was increased. The stability of these patterns and their relation to patterns of inferencing in the linguistic mode remains to be established.

INFERENCING IN FOREIGN LANGUAGE LEARNING: CUES AND THEIR FUNCTIONS

A tripartite taxonomy of cues was established to facilitate the exploration of the functions of cues in inferencing in foreign language learning. This taxonomy was organized around the fact that in language study it is: (1) the nature of the target language; (2) its relation to the background language (or other languages known to the learner); and (3) the 'content' of messages, or linguistic material, under consideration that determine the possibilities for making inferences. Thus the descriptors *intra-lingual*, *inter-lingual* and *extra-lingual* were suggested for categorizing cues.

Intra-lingual cues are supplied by the target language. The student who uses them must, of course, have some knowledge of the target language. Essentially intra-lingual cues occur in the morphological and syntactic regularity of the language.

Intra-lingual cues are particularly useful in identifying the form class of a novel term. Thus cues such as specific pluralizing markers applicable only to nouns, tense markers applicable only to verbs, or word order constraints of a given language will fall into this category. Although identification of a form class does not, in itself, constitute a complete recognition of a novel term, it may go a long way toward reducing the possible number of inferences that can be made. Identification of form classes increases the certainty of inferencing and it affects the complexity of the inference situation. Furthermore, the use of such cues makes it possible to generate searches for additional contextual material and it seems reasonable to hypothesize that they may stimulate and accelerate the student's further exploration of the text rather than allow the unfamiliar term to distract his attention from the text and hinder his progress with it.

Some additional kinds of intra-lingual cues of a completely structural nature are, for example, markers of grammatical gender or of 'animate' and 'inanimate' nouns which a number of languages exhibit. There is, of course, much justified argument holding that in many instances these are purely grammatical, or structural, phenomena that are not at all semantic. Synchronic linguistics may remain somewhat puzzled as to the present function of such markers. But it is reasonable to suppose that these markers did once correspond to semantic categories and that their statistical reliability – or their 'regularity' – was diminished by the vicissitudes of linguistic change. These markers, therefore, retain potential usefulness as cues for making reasonable, if probabilistic, guesses when coupled with other cues. Thus purported attributes of masculinity or femininity may not be very reliable in helping us decide whether we ought to put *le* or *la* before *table* in French nor may the marker go very far in helping us decide what *table* (when known to be a noun that follows *la*) may mean. Yet in a context in which a specific kinship relationship is described, the presence of *la* before *mère* might quite unequivocally suggest that mother and not father is implied.

Intra-lingual cues are not exclusively grammatical or structural. In many languages semantic implications may be frequently suggested by derivational affixes and transparent stems functioning in concert. In English, for example, there are many productive, but bound, morphemes that suggest notions such as 'agent' (*-or* or *-er*), 'abstraction' (*-tion*), 'having the property of' (*-ive*), etc. Knowledge of a group of suffixes such as these can narrow the semantic field in respect to the notions they suggest. Furthermore, when such suffixes appear connected to a stem which the student may have encountered elsewhere, the specific meaning of a novel vocable is completely suggested. Thus, a first encounter with *operative* may present little problem for a student who already knows the meaning of *operator*, *operation* and *adjustive*. Agglutinating languages and languages that make regular use of stems which remain relatively transparent (such as the Semitic languages) would seem to be particularly well suited to inferencing upon this type of morphological cue. Indeed, at the level of recognizing novel combinations of productive bound morphemes, inferencing may be said to overlap with the utilization of the generative property of language in comprehension.

A relatively unexplored domain of intra-lingual cues is the phenomenon associated with phonesthemes. Phonesthemes are consonant clusters that seem to be related to a semantic category. For example, there are indications that English words containing initial /sl/ fall into fourteen meaning categories, some of which are weakness, sloppiness, slowness, etc.[1] Other phonesthemes in English seem to be /sp/ for radiating explosions from limited sources, /fl/ which seems to be related to flowing motions, and /bl/ which seems to be related to explosions. A limited analysis of phonesthemes has, to date, apparently been conducted on a purely linguistic basis, and beyond some conjecture in psychology,[2] the related psychological phenomena have not been completely explored. The question as to whether phonesthemes may be used in inferencing to reduce universes of possible meanings and to suggest possible meanings remains to be answered. The dangers that attention to phonesthemes might nurture tendencies toward erroneous 'homophonic word realism' are also to be kept in mind.

The category of *inter-lingual cues* includes all the possible derivations that may be made on the basis of loans between languages, the occurrence of cognates, and the occurrence of regularities of phonological transformations from one language to another. The usefulness of this category of cues would suggest that a few minutes of instruction on Grimm's law – which describes the correspondences of certain consonants in High Germanic languages, with other consonants in Low Germanic languages – may prove to be very profitable for the English speaking student of German.

The usefulness of the category of inter-lingual cues is, of course, contingent upon historical relations and contacts between the target language and the native language of the student. There are interesting subtleties to these interrelations which might have valuable implications for curricular decisions about language study; questions such as the selection of a language that one or another pupil might most profitably

---

[1] Carton (1956).
[2] Skinner (1957). A rather large array of studies deals with 'phonetic symbolism' which may prove to be a phenomenon closely related to the phonestheme and have similar implications for inferencing.

study, when he should study it, and how it may be relevant to the remainder of his curriculum.

In the context of research on The 'Method of Inference' in foreign language study some selected texts in German and French were cursorily studied for the relative proportion of words that might be inferenceable on the basis of inter-lingual cues by English speaking students.[1] The most preliminary of examinations revealed a phenomenon that is amply explained in any standard history of the English language, namely, that German cognates with English are essentially in the domain of 'household' or everyday vocabulary while cognates with French occur in the technical, learned, esthetic, and academic domains. Thus (though systematic empirical proof is yet lacking) it may well be that the rapidity by which skill in comprehending French is acquired may be enhanced by a few years of academic study in the background of the pupil; study which is not quite as relevant to the acquisition of skill in comprehending German.

Inter-lingual cues and some intra-lingual cues require attention directly upon the novel term. If inferencing with them were to proceed without concurrent attention to other cues, they would expose the student to possible errors analogous to 'homophonic word realism.' Indeed, the famous 'false friends' that have for so long in the history of foreign language pedagogy justified the memorization of vocabulary lists may be seen as generating errors that are akin to homophonic word realism.

A modest study, in which eighth and ninth grade students in their first or second year of French study participated, revealed, however, that the dangers of incorrect inferencing are not as severe as might be feared. The groups of students in this experiment were required to provide English equivalents to lists of French words and expressions which they had not previously encountered in their curriculum. Depending upon the sophistication of the group, the means of correct responses to lists of words ranged from 27 to 47 per cent correct for one list and from 14 to 30 per cent correct for a second list.

Next, the students were given a passage of French to read which was at an appropriate level of difficulty for them and which contained the words they had been asked to identify. The students were then asked to identify the words in the lists a second time. In five out of seven test administrations there were clear increases in the number of words and

[1] Carton (1966). This document contains exhaustive descriptions of the experiments referred to in this paper.

expressions correctly identified although the particular lists and the passages played a role in the nature of the results. In the sixth and seventh instances no appreciable changes in either direction were found.

The means of numbers of wrong responses in the first administration ran somewhat higher than the number of right responses. These means ranged from 45 to 51 per cent wrong for the first list and from 53 to 61 per cent wrong for the second list. There were *no* instances in which the means of wrong responses did not decrease after exposure to the reading passages with the differences between the first and second means ranging from a mere 2·5 percentage points to as much as 31 percentage points. In general, changes in wrong responses from the first set of responses to the second set were either to right responses or to omissions.

The design of the study was somewhat more complex than the results reported here would suggest. Nevertheless, the data relevant to the issue at hand clearly suggest that relatively young pupils can not only make extensive use of inter-lingual cues (and some intra-lingual ones) but they can also make good use of context cues (or extra-lingual cues) to correct misapprehensions.

In one instance (not included in the data discussed above) one group did not respond to the list of words prior to reading the passage because of an error in administering the experiment. In this group the mean of wrong responses was lower than for any of the other groups (23 per cent) after they had read the passage. There were also other indications found in the available data of a tendency for wrong guesses to persist after they are made. This tendency was noted also by observers in the classroom and indications of it were found in the studies involving the Visual Inference Test. Thus, despite the evidence which bespeaks a high level of flexibility and ability to readjust to new cues on the part of the subjects participating in these experiments, it would seem advisable in pedagogy to avoid presenting terms for inferencing in isolation. Since students are apparently able to utilize considerable diversity of cues for correct inferencing, the presentation of novel terms in cue-rich contexts apparently minimizes errors. Since there is a tendency for errors to persist, it is obviously wise to forestall their occurrence. It is probably wiser still to devote at least some pedagogic energies to enhance the flexibility of students and their abilities to correct themselves, although it must be admitted that the techniques for such pedagogy are not as yet in wide use in foreign language instruction.

Extra-lingual, or contextual, cues derive their usefulness essentially from the fact that an important function of language is to represent objects and events in the 'real world.' When we talk, we quite frequently talk about something. Regularities in the objective world we talk about make it possible for us to expect many occurrences in it. If we can sometimes predict the occurrences of the real world, it follows that we can sometimes predict the words, or the meanings of the words, that represent these occurrences.

The descriptions of Cloze procedure and the Word-Context Test illustrated the fact that respondents may be completely dependent upon extra-lingual cues and function effectively. Studies in which reading passages were introduced to supplement and change responses made exclusively on the basis of intra-lingual and inter-lingual cues illustrated the fact that cues can function in concert.

The student of a foreign language that is widely divergent from his native language is very largely dependent on extra-lingual cues (and upon intra-lingual cues only after he has acquired some proficiency). Since utterances and texts in widely divergent languages are likely to be descriptive of widely divergent cultures and 'real worlds,' texts containing extra-lingual cues valuable to the learner may be difficult to obtain, rendering the study of a divergent language all the more difficult. The student of a divergent language is probably well advised to be a student of the culture of that language. If he is, much of his inferencing will be coupled with concept attainment.

In a seventh grade class an experimenter undertook to explain how extra-lingual cues might profitably be used to recognize unfamiliar words in a text. After practicing a few examples, a number of the pupils spontaneously noted that the more experience and knowledge one had, the more competent one was likely to be at inferencing; that the more one knew, the more one was likely to learn.

There are two aspects of inferencing which remain essentially *terra incognita* despite the fact that it would seem that a complete understanding of them would be crucial to an effective pedagogy utilizing inferencing. These aspects are complexity and certainty. Examples of questions that might be explored analytically and experimentally under the rubric of complexity are the following. What is the effect of the number of cues upon an inferencing situation? Are there differences in the 'valences' or salience of the various kinds of cues? What are the implications for the respondent of various mixes? What are the implications of a set of cues that are congruent in the solution they suggest as opposed to sets of cues that suggest divergent solutions? In general, these questions imply that more information is needed to understand how students might use cues and cope with the diversity of cues that they may have to contend with.

In studying certainty, a distinction is to be made between subjective certainty and objective certainty. Either descriptive linguistics or the statistical study of language can provide empirical statements about the probabilities of the occurrence of a given linguistic unit in specified contexts. Yet respondents' perceptions may or may not coincide with the empirical data. Objective certainty may justify ready inferencing, but subjective certainty may be expected to determine ready inferencing. How can subjective and objective certainty be made to coincide? An interesting finding in respect to the *Visual Inference Test* along these lines was the tendency of subjects to report higher certainty in respect to correct guesses than in respect to incorrect guesses although they showed a very marked tendency to report greater certainty in respect to guesses based on many cues than in respect to guesses based on few cues, irrespective of whether their guesses were correct or incorrect. Finally, a psychology of inferencing is to be expected to establish the relations and interactions between certainty and complexity.

CONCLUSION

For many students the process designated as inferencing already undoubtedly comprises part of their strategies for learning and using language. Some foreign language pedagogy has long been cognizant of the process. The proposal to introduce extensive use of the process represents, however, a sharp departure from those views of language study which put exclusive emphasis on mimicry and memory and which leave little room for doubtfulness and temporary inaccuracies.

Pedagogic strategies which put extensive emphasis on providing models for monitored memorization imply to the student that responsibility for all they will need to know has been assumed by the formal setting for learning. When emphasis is placed upon processes of acquisition, the student is prepared for independent study and may be expected to continue to extend his command over the subject matter after leaving formal instruction.

A program of research on inferencing in language must attend to both the psychological nature of the process and to language as an ecology in which it can be manifested. Thus a basic perceptual and cognitive process is to be examined for: (1) the manner in which it operates; (2) the effect of various circumstances upon its operation; (3) the possible factors that might cause the process to become dysfunctional; and (4) the natural course of development of the functioning of the process in the maturing individual. Such research may be expected to eventuate in a family of pedagogic procedures for nurturing the process and enhancing the skill that students might exhibit in applying it.

The view of language which is attendant upon the utilization of inferencing is that many linguistic events are probabilistic and that comprehension is enhanced by intuitions into contingencies. The influence of 'information theory' upon this formulation is obvious. While the futility of a purely statistical description of language as an approach to generating and comprehending meaningful sentences is not to be denied, it is argued here that it is precisely the perception of probabilistically contingent relations (both in language and in respect to the 'content' of messages) that enhances and provides possibilities for the selection of appropriate linguistic units in production and the correct interpretation of these units in comprehension. The research into language generated by an interest in inferencing is concerned, therefore, with how linguistic units and the structures of sentences and paragraphs provide cues for the interpretation of other linguistic units.

The view that language production and perception are largely dependent on the psychological processing of probabilistically contingent cues is implicit in the taxonomy of cues presented here. The assertion that cues from various echelons and levels of discourse are made to function in concert is a major underpinning of the psycholinguistic theory from which a research program on inferencing might be derived.

The possibilities of the wide generality of such a theory are not to be overlooked (although they cannot be fully developed in the context of the present paper). For example, homophony and the appearances of utterances with identical surface structures and differing deep structures are frequent occurrences. A theory of language inferencing might suggest that the correct interpretation of such utterances depends on the adequate processing of probabilistic contingencies of events to be found at extra-lingual echelons.

A language pedagogy that utilizes inferencing removes language study from the domain of mere skills to a domain that is more closely akin to the regions of complex intellectual processes. Language study becomes a matter for a kind of problem-solving and the entire breadth of the student's experience and knowledge may be brought to bear on the processing of language. A distinction between language and thought – which is valuable for the analysis and study of how each develops – is abandoned, in dealing with students who can already both think and use language, in favor of a view that sees the processing of language as one of many forms of thought and which allows for the possibility that language processing and other forms of thinking may occur concurrently. A distinction between a linguistic level and a content level in messages – which is valuable for analyzing and clarifying the nature of language – is abandoned in the context of language comprehension in favor of a view holding that, psychologically, comprehension may depend on the concurrent processing of cues from several echelons.

BIBLIOGRAPHY

Boring, E. G. *A history of experimental psychology.* 2nd ed. New York: Appleton-Century-Crofts, 1950.
Carroll, J. B., Carton, A. S., and Wilds, Claudia P. *An investigation of 'Cloze' items in the measurement of achievement in foreign languages.* Research Development Reports, College Entrance Examination Board. Cambridge, Mass.: Laboratory for Research in Instruction, Harvard University, 1959.
Carton, A. S. *Initial/sl/in English.* Diss., Columbia University, 1956.
    Report of Phase 1 of testing for the Russian Summer Language Program. Mimeographed work paper, Inter-University Committee on Travel Grants, 1959.
    The 'Method of Inference' in foreign language study. Mimeo. New York: Division of Teacher Education of the City University of New York, 1966.
Chomsky, Noam. *Language and mind.* New York: Harcourt, Brace and World, 1968.
Ebbinghaus, H. 'Ueber eine neue Methode zur Prufung geistiger Fähigkeiten und ihre Anwendung bei Schulkindern.' *Zeitschrift für Psychologie*, **13** (1897), 401–59.
Goodman, K. S., and Fleming, J. T. (eds.). *Psycholinguistics and the teaching of reading.* Newark, Del.: International Reading Association, 1969.
Lenneberg, E. 'The natural history of language.' In Smith and Miller, *The genesis of language*, pp. 219–52.
McNeill, D. 'Developmental psycholinguistics'. In Smith and Miller, *The genesis of language*, pp. 15–84.
Skinner, B. F. *Verbal behavior.* New York: Appleton-Century-Crofts, 1957.
Smith, F., and Miller, G. A. *The genesis of language: a psycholinguistic approach.* Cambridge, Mass.: M.I.T. Press, 1966.
Taylor, W. L. 'Cloze procedure: a new tool for measuring readability.' *Journalism Quarterly*, **33** (1953), 42–8.
    'Cloze readability scores as indices of individual differences in comprehension and aptitude.' *Journal of Applied Psychology*, **41** (1957), 19–26.
Vigotsky, L. S. *Thought and language.* Cambridge, Mass.: M.I.T. Press, 1962.
Werner, H., and Kaplan, B. *Symbol formation.* New York: Wiley, 1963.

6 *Sociopsychological problems in language mastery and retention*

EUGENE A. NIDA

Much significant research has been applied to the problems of learning a first language, and perhaps even more has been expended on the difficulties of second-language learning.[1] Most of these investigations have concentrated upon various aspects of the psychology of learning, though some have also dealt with other, and perhaps to some extent more fundamental, problems, namely motivation, language prejudice, and 'language shock' as one of the aspects of 'culture shock.'[2]

Relatively little research, however, has been related to three other aspects of language mastery and use: (1) failure of some persons to learn a foreign language, despite continued and excellent exposure, (2) leveling off in the process of language learning, despite continued exposure, and (3) significant declines in ability to use a language which has once been moderately well learned or even mastered. Though certain of these problems may seem quite tangential to the principal interests of many persons concerned with language teaching, nevertheless it is quite possible that the insights gained from a careful consideration of these types of difficulties in language mastery and use may suggest important new approaches to some of the nagging problems with which we are constantly so concerned.

The following discussion of language learning problems is not, how-ever, based upon psychological tests with control groups or upon broad surveys. In the first place, the problems which are presented here do not lend themselves readily to psychological testing; and in the second place, there is as yet no large body of data on which one might draw for comparison. Nevertheless, it does seem that the types of problems which are presented here are much more likely to yield to explanations based

[1] Brooks (1960), Carroll (1964), Jakobovits and Miron (1967), Moulton (1961).
[2] Larson and Smalley (1970).

59

upon tests of psychological profiles than are the problems encountered in the average classroom situation. The learning difficulties of people outside the classroom are much closer to real-life situations and thus more likely to reflect fundamental psychological traits and predispositions than do those problems which one encounters in attempts to test such personality features as related to classroom performance.

FAILURE TO LEARN A SECOND LANGUAGE DESPITE CONTINUED EXPOSURE

We are all aware of some persons who have lived in a foreign country for many years and have successfully resisted all the seemingly natural influences which would have produced a competent speaker of a second language. The experience of a New York lawyer with extensive professional interests in Latin America may serve to illustrate a number of the factors which are involved in such situations. This man is a highly successful person, who has lived in Latin America for a number of years and who maintains a large office in one of the important capitals. He knows Latin American law and is very competent in reading Spanish – in fact, he not only knows what is said, but recognizes what is not said. Furthermore, he can follow conversations in Spanish with complete ease and uncanny insight. But despite all of this knowledge and exposure, he cannot utter a sentence in Spanish without atrocious pronunciation and incredibly bad grammar. He depends constantly upon an assistant to serve as his interpreter. What is more, he does not hesitate to apologize for his utterly inadequate use of Spanish. But in his ready willingness to apologize, he also reveals that his interpreter is a prestige symbol and serves to keep Latin Americans at a distance – something which seems so important to his not-too-well-disguised sense of superiority.

This lawyer exhibits an almost incredible gap between the passive (or consumer) language and the active (or producer) language. Mastery of the consumer aspects of the language, i.e. ability to understand, has been essential and hence he has become highly efficient. However, inability to master the producer aspects of the language has been likewise highly motivated. As a result the discrepancies between these two phases of language use are sociologically striking and psychologically important.

Failure to learn a language may, however, occur at the opposite end of the social scale. An Aztec Indian woman in the village of Tetelcingo, Morelos, Mexico, had lived extensively in a Spanish setting, but she had seemingly no conscious control of the language, neither in hearing nor in speaking. However, when she was drunk at a fiesta she could reel off Spanish with excellent pronunciation and correct grammar. From the nature of the content she was obviously not just reciting something which had been memorized. There may be a number of different explanations of this phenomenon, but it would seem that perhaps the most reasonable explanation is simply that she had accepted the 'role of the dumb Indian' – a role imposed upon her by the Spanish-speaking persons for whom she had worked. Furthermore, she was obviously basically resentful of the Spanish-speaking society and hence in self-defense refused to identify with this society to the extent of conscious control of the language.

There are some instances in which failure in language learning has obvious immediate economic advantages, which may figure in one's decision not to speak a foreign language. One international oil operator in the Middle East insists that he can get a better deal if he makes people speak to him in English rather than attempting to speak to them in Arabic. An American business man in Bangkok continues to speak only English, since he finds that when he goes into government offices his inability to use Thai means that he is referred to the higher officials who speak English – the very ones with whom he wants to talk.

Illustrative examples, such as the lawyer in Latin America and the Indian woman in Mexico, could be repeated almost endlessly, and in each instance there are certain conscious or unconscious motivations which act as blocks to language assimilation and use. Basically, however, these factors are perhaps not significantly different from those which influence a student to conclude that he simply cannot learn a foreign language, largely because he does not want to.

LEVELING OFF IN LANGUAGE LEARNING

In some respects the leveling off in language performance, despite continued exposure, is even more striking and complex than failure to learn in the first place. Such a leveling off process may take place within a few weeks or months after the student has completed language school abroad, or it may occur within a couple of years, but in a high percentage of cases most learning, both in the consumer and producer aspects of the language, tends to stop once the 'initiation rites' have been completed. By 'initiation rites' we mean either the formal examinations (language learning by many persons stops immediately after exams), or the degree of acceptance within the foreign language community which seems necessary for carrying on one's activities with minimal effort.

Early leveling off in language competence usually reflects simply intellectual laziness on the part of the foreign-language learner. But there may be other important contributing factors. In the first place, he may never have realized that one can learn a foreign language outside of the classroom context. The idea that one can learn by merely listening seems utterly incredible to some people. In the second place, he may not have gained sufficient competence in the second language so as to feel at ease in conversations, and hence he instinctively avoids contacts which would tend to improve his language ability. Lastly, in his work, social contacts, and household, he may be surrounded by people who are willing to adjust to his relatively low level of language performance. This is often true, for example, in mission station compounds and in embassy offices. In fact, people may be entirely too kind. For example, some German employers of Italians in Germany speak to their workers with an Italian accent in order to make sure that the people understand. But this does not help the Italians to learn German. Precisely the same type of thing occurs in mission stations, army posts, embassies, and mining compounds around the world.

Persons who level off in language learning within a couple of years after completing formal study of a language tend to do so when they reach a point where they think their use of the language represents maximal impact for minimal effort. At about this same time those who surround such learners are also likely to give up in making demands upon them, either by correcting their usage or by seeming not to understand. In other words, there is a point of mutual adjustment where further demands from the foreign-language community seem like wasted effort, and where further effort on the part of the second-language learner appears to be out of proportion to what he is likely to accomplish. This point of mutual adjustment may be quite low, as for example in the case of an American housewife who gets by with 'kitchen Arabic' in a petroleum center. It may be quite high, as in the case of foreign attachés. The level is often dependent upon one's status, for the higher the status the lower the level tends to be. For example, Belgians in the Congo level off in their use of African languages at a much lower level than do the Portuguese. The Belgians are in more dominant positions and therefore can expect a greater effort on the part of others to adjust to them.

Tolerance for a relatively low level of language performance is often surprisingly great, especially if the speaker exhibits utter sincerity of purpose. In fact, one American woman in Mexico has had unusual success in various humanitarian projects, in some measure because she is rather inadequate in Spanish. She is, however, so utterly open, generous, and sincere that government officials almost inevitably identify with her. When she attempts to present her case in her rather fantastic Spanish (with fairly good pronunciation but utterly impossible grammar), government officials soon find themselves helping her out with her appeals, thus making her requests their own. The grammatical structure of this woman's speech is quite inadequate, but her paralinguistic features are superb, and she is very successful.

In some situations the use of language at a level below standard may be consciously contrived, rather than the result of failure to advance. For example, before independence some Anglo-Indians purposely spoke Hindi incorrectly so as to symbolize what they regarded as their superior status. In South Africa many persons of English background maintain a very low level of Afrikaans as a way of demonstrating their class consciousness.

In dealing with problems of leveling off in language performance, one must generally make a clear distinction between the consumer and producer aspects of language. A person may continue to increase his ability to understand, while remaining at a relatively fixed level in his ability to speak. Similarly, he may improve his reading capacity, while remaining quite limited in his ability to write. Nevertheless, many persons level off in both the consumer and producer aspects of the language. In short, their capacity ossifies.

From the standpoint of the second-language learning the leveling off process normally involves three different sociopsychological elements in various combinations and proportions: (1) intellectual fatigue (a more sophisticated way of speaking about people being mentally lazy), (2) no feeling for the need of greater identification with the surrounding community, and (3) the conviction that further effort will not produce compensatory results. For people in the surrounding foreign language community motivations for mutual adjustment include: (1) the loss of hope that the learner is likely to improve, (2) the greater ease in adjusting to the learner's lower level than in attempting to teach him to advance, and (3) the advantage of keeping such a person relatively isolated and thus in a position where he can be more readily controlled. When, as in all interpersonal behavior, 'information is power,' there are always some advantages in seeing that certain persons remain dependent upon others for information.

DECLINE IN LANGUAGE ABILITY

It is not difficult to understand the processes by which an individual may decline in language ability if he is removed from constant exposure. Such a decline is especially rapid in the case of a second language, and is particularly so if the language has been only partially learned. Such a decline may even occur in the case of one's own mother tongue. For example, Europeans who have immigrated to America frequently decline radically in their capacity to use their mother tongue. Furthermore, they often do not learn English well, so that they ultimately end up without any language in which they can adequately express themselves.

What is, however, much more surprising is that one may decline in language ability even with continuous exposure. When a person ceases to listen actively to a foreign language, he usually begins a relatively rapid decline in his correct handling of the grammar. If he stops his reading in the language, often with the excuse that he is too busy, his consumer and producer ability in the language may decline. One very obvious reason for decline is a radical shift of interest. For example, as soon as a person receives a notice of transfer to some other language area, a decline in language competence often takes place.

Another reason for decline in language performance may involve a shift in communication role. For example, when a person is shifted from a position of receiving or transmitting information to one in which he is the censor of information, i.e. when he is given a top administrative position, his capacity in the language may suffer decline. In a position of authority he seemingly does not feel so compelled to listen, since others must listen to him. Moreover, he is not obliged to follow conversations, but usually directs them. Furthermore, much of the information which he receives to guide him in his work reaches him in his own mother tongue rather than in the local language. This likewise has a deleterious effect upon his capacity in the foreign language.

Many persons decline in producer capacity, i.e. in ability to speak and write, while increasing in consumer capacity. Though one normally assumes that these capacities are very closely related and mutually supporting, this is by no means always the case.

One other factor or set of factors which may institute a rapid decline in capacity is the fear of not being really successful in language mastery. This may institute a severe crisis in the learning process, with the result that a person gives up entirely and begins a very abrupt decline in performance.

LANGUAGE MASTERY AND USE

The study of the problems involved in language learning beyond the stage of the classroom or the textbook deserves much greater attention than it has received in the past, since the problems are much more complex than they have often been described as being. The context of such learning is essentially unstructured, that is to say, it is not organized around set hours, systematic steps in learning, or appropriate tests. Moreover, the factors are quite variable, both with respect to the motivations of the learner as well as to circumstances of learning.

The study of such post-classroom factors in language learning is, however, exceedingly important, not only as a means of helping people organize their later learning with greater efficiency, but also as a program for analyzing the basic problems of language learning, even in the classroom, in terms of the broader context of language mastery and use.

BIBLIOGRAPHY

Brooks, Nelson. *Language and language learning: theory and practice.* 2nd ed. New York: Harcourt, Brace, and World, 1964.
Carroll, J. B. *Language and thought.* Englewood Cliffs. N.J.: Prentice-Hall, 1964.
Jakobovits, Leon A., and Miron, M. S. (eds.). *Readings in the psychology of language.* Englewood Cliffs, N. J.: Prentice-Hall, 1967.
Larson, Donald N., and Smalley, William A. *Becoming bilingual: a guide to language learning.* Richmond, Va.: Foreign Missions Board of the Southern Baptist Convention, 1970.
Moulton, William G. 'Linguistics and language teaching in the United States 1940–1960.' In Mohrmann, Ch., Sommerfelt, A., and Whatmough, J. *Trends in European and American linguistics 1930–1960.* Utrecht: Spectrum, 1961.

7 *Mastery learning and foreign languages*

REBECCA M. VALETTE

PART I: THE PROBLEM

We American language teachers must face up to an unpleasant truth: most of the students who begin language study in our classes fail to attain a level of basic competence in a second language. Language study is often considered simply as an unpleasant hurdle standing between the student and college entrance or the acquisition of an advanced academic degree.

Recent research has corroborated the existence of an unhealthy situation in foreign language instruction in the United States.

Attrition. In an address to the Massachusetts Foreign Language Association, Dwight Allen castigated the profession for the high attrition rate in the secondary schools. Paul Pimsleur and his team (1966) pointed out that roughly 20% of the foreign language students in a large midwestern city could be classified as underachievers, that is, these students had language grades which were one grade-point lower than their major subject average. They found an attrition rate of about 50% after one year of instruction and 90% after three years.

Attitude. In the final Pennsylvania report on the effectiveness of three approaches to foreign language teaching and three language laboratory systems, Philip Smith (1970) underlines the general *decline* in attitude over a two-year period of both the better and the poorer high school students.

Failure to learn. Newmark (1966) reports on a California study with elementary students of Spanish in which three different teaching methods (classroom instruction, TV instruction and programmed instruction) were being evaluated. Since the programs each contained somewhat different objectives, and since there were differences in the lexicon and grammar being taught, the research team decided to construct three separate criterion-referenced tests, each based on the content and objectives of one of the teaching methods. A striking finding of this project was that, regardless of method, students were not mastering the objectives of the language course in which they were enrolled. All three methods were more or less producing failures. (The one positive feature of the study was that the team established the feasibility of using criterion-referenced tests on a large scale.) John B. Carroll (1967) upon measuring the linguistic preparation of foreign-language majors at the college level by means of the MLA Proficiency Test for Teachers and Advanced Students, noted the generally low median levels of attainment in the audio-lingual skills.

When we foreign language teachers are confronted with our failure, we frequently seek refuge behind four 'excuses':

1. 'But look at my star pupils X and Y: they have attained near-native fluency even though they have not had the opportunity to travel abroad.' Unfortunately the existence of a handful of successful students in no way compensates for our failure to teach the remaining 90%. That successful handful would probably have been able to attain that level of fluency without us. And furthermore, nobody doubts that language teachers have occasionally transmitted their knowledge to a select few, or else they would never have been able to perpetuate the priesthood of language teachers.

2. 'Many students just haven't received the proper preparation before they enter my class. They don't know how to study. They don't even know anything about their own language.' Of course, none of us would deny the benefits of solid academic background for each of our students. But the whole concept of education is based on the premise that the teacher accepts the 'raw material' he is given, that is, the students with their strengths and with their weaknesses, and brings these students several steps forward on the path of learning. This is the challenge of teaching.

3. 'Students haven't been able to learn the second language because they have been taught by Method X. Were we all to use Method Y, then our students would really be able to master the language.' This excuse is widespread and the name of any method (traditional, audio-lingual, direct, etc.) may be inserted in slots X and Y, depending on who is

making the statement. Every few years the vogue changes and teachers clamber on a new bandwagon, confident that salvation (that is, success in teaching a language) is around the corner. Yet the method, of itself, is only one factor in student learning: some students have been successfully taught by each of the current methods, but most students have typically experienced failure.

4. 'A lot of my students simply lack language aptitude.' This argument is probably the most pernicious, and even though the 'special language gift' myth and its corollary the 'language block' have never been corroborated by research many students, administrators, and teachers keep pretending they exist. It's a fine 'out' for all concerned, for Johnny's failure to learn is then neither the teacher's fault, nor the school's fault, nor his own fault: his failure was inevitable.

Our excuses are obviously not valid. But where shall we look for a remedy to our widespread failure to teach foreign languages?

PART II: TEACHER EXPECTANCIES

An important component in student success is the teacher's mental set. If one teacher expects all of his students to master the French sound system, they usually do, whereas if another teacher is convinced that most students will never get it, his students usually do not. Recent research by Rosenthal and Jacobsen (1968) confirms the self-fulfilling nature of teacher expectancies. In September the teachers of a California elementary school were told that certain students would probably spurt ahead in intelligence as signaled by their performance on a new type of 'prognostic' intelligence test administered the previous spring. Actually the test had no predictive qualities and the names of the potential spurters had been chosen at random. In May of that academic year an administration of the same intelligence test revealed that the 'spurters', especially in the lower grades, actually showed significant increases in measured IQ and that these increases were particularly marked in the case of the 'more Mexican' children. Apparently the teachers must have first been surprised to note the presence of 'spurters' among their less promising students and then, in some way, unknowingly communicated to the children that they anticipated better intellectual performance. Were language teachers to expect all students to master a second language, we might well experience greater success.

PART III: MASTERY LEARNING

In mastery learning the teacher insists that all students attain specific lesson objectives before introducing the next unit. Let us turn our attention for a moment to Carroll's (1962) learning model. Success, or mastery of a task, is seen as the function of five factors:

instructional factors—

    presentation of material (text, teacher, etc.)
    time allowed for learning

student factors—

    general intelligence (ability to follow instructions)
    motivation (degree of perseverance)
    aptitude (time needed for learning)

It is interesting to note here that aptitude is defined as an individual's learning rate: in other words, all students (except the mentally deficient) can learn a second language, but some will learn more rapidly than others. Bloom (1968) has taken Carroll's model and placed the emphasis on success. He insists that we must change our instructional system so that we lead each student through a sequence of successful learning experiences: we must vary the types of presentations and the time allowed for learning so as to permit all students to attain a degree of mastery.

Why is mastery learning so important in language teaching? Since foreign language learning at the early levels is cumulative and highly sequential (a feature emphasized by the Pimsleur underachievement study), it is essential that a student not be 'pushed' through a course of instruction, but rather be allowed to master the program lesson by lesson.

Why cannot programmed courses remedy the situation? One reason conventional programmed courses have not proven as effective as was once hoped is that the modern foreign languages are taught as communication skills. Communication requires the interaction of individuals. Thus it seems that a certain amount of classroom speaking practice is essential in all classes.

How can mastery learning be implemented in the classroom? One way, which is currently being used in many American schools is teaching by ability and achievement grouping. Hernick and Kennedy (1968) report that an effective system of multi-level grouping can reduce attrition and increase student motivation.

Melvin Smith (1968) directed an experiment to determine whether criterion-referenced tests might not be effectively used to improve classroom instruction during the school year. Since the results of this piece of research bear directly on our problem (how to bring more students to the point where they truly learn a second language), we shall describe the findings in some detail.

Teachers of sixth-grade Spanish (all using A–LM materials) were divided into three groups. Before and after each unit of instruction, all classes were given a criterion-referenced listening-comprehension test based on the material in the text. Teachers in Group 3 (No Responsibility) were not informed of the results of the test and proceeded at their own individual pace. Teachers in Group 2 (Informed but not Responsible) were given the test results but did not receive special instructions about how to act on the information; typically they went on to the next unit once the final criterion-referenced test had been administered. Teachers in Group 1 (Specific Responsiblity) were not only told the test results, but were *not* permitted to continue to the next unit until 90% of the students were able to respond correctly to 80% of the items. At the end of the year, Group 2 and 3 had finished three units, whereas Group 1 was only half way through unit three. All groups were administered the final unit three test, Group 1 performed significantly better than the other two groups and made the highest gains between the pretest and the posttest. The report concludes:

> Using criterion-referenced tests to indicate pupil achievement of specific objectives and teaching to these objectives is a significantly better way of teaching than
>
> (a) using criterion-referenced tests to indicate pupil achievement but not teaching to specific objectives
>
> (b) not using criterion-referenced tests and not being responsible for specific objectives.

Results on the posttest showed that:

Scores above 85% increased 10-fold when teachers were specifically responsible.

Failures were reduced by 44% when teachers were specifically responsible.

Individual gains were 33% higher when teachers were specifically responsible.

71

Finally, it was determined that teachers who are held specifically responsible for the performance of their students become 1.6 times more effective in teaching the foreign language.

In larger schools, criterion-referenced testing and the assumption of specific responsibility can be paired with a track system. The better students move ahead as a group (90% of the students mastering at least 80% of the material) while the slower students progress at a rate suited to their learning speed.

PART IV: THE CORE CONCEPT AS APPLIED TO TEACHING
MATERIALS

The core concept facilitates the implementation of a mastery learning strategy in the classroom and permits individualized instruction and self-pacing. In essence, each unit or lesson is conceived as containing a core segment of basic structures and lexicon which all students are expected to master. The lesson may also contain some other expressions or lexical items which are classified as non-core. Cognates, for example, may be introduced for recognition and be considered non-core. Since the slower learners will spend more time mastering the core material, supplementary materials are available for the faster learners. Such materials may consist of listening-comprehension tapes (where the core material plus cognates are recombined into selections recorded at varied rates of delivery) and reading-comprehension passages. In the classroom, provision might be made to have the faster students tutor those who are experiencing difficulty with certain aspects of the lesson. Since the entire class progresses as a group from lesson to lesson, all students may participate in conversation activities. At the same time, however, students will be working individually or in small groups on other segments of the lesson material. Thus, the core is the key to unity in the classroom, and the supplementary components allow for individualization and diversity. Each student will be given the opportunity to master a second language.

Mastery learning techniques of themselves will not remedy the unhealthy situation of foreign-language instruction in the United States. Positive teacher expectancies are crucial. Adequate learning materials and creative teaching are further requisites. But there is nothing quite so heady as success: once entire classes realize they are actually mastering a second language rather than being slowly engulfed by the rising tide of incomprehension, motivation will increase, attitudes will improve, and students will finally be *learning* a new language rather than just 'studying' it.

BIBLIOGRAPHY

Bloom, Benjamin S. 'Learning for mastery.' *UCLA Evaluation Comment*, **1**, 2 (1968).
Carroll, John B. 'The prediction of success in intensive foreign language training.' In Glaser, 1962.
  'Foreign language proficiency levels attained by language majors near graduation from college.' *Foreign Language Annals*, **1** (1967), 131–51.
Glaser, Robert (ed.). *Training research and education*. Pittsburgh: University of Pittsburgh Press, 1962. (Reprinted by MLA Materials Center.)
Hernick, Michael, and Kennedy, Dora. 'Multi-level grouping of students in the modern foreign language program.' *Foreign Language Annals*. **2** (1968), 200–4.
Newmark, Gerald *et al. A field test of three approaches to the teaching of Spanish in elementary schools*. Sacramento, Calif.: California State Department of Education, 1966.
Pimsleur, Paul, Sundland, Donald M., and McIntyre, Ruth D. *Under-achievement in foreign language learning*. New York: MLA, 1966.
Rosenthal, Robert, and Jacobsen, Lenore F. *Pygmalion in the classroom*. New York: Holt, Rinehart and Winston, 1968.
Smith, Melvin I. *Teaching to specific objectives*. Modesto, Calif.: Stanislaus County Schools Office, 1968.
Smith, Philip D., Jr. *A comparison of the cognitive and audiolingual approaches to foreign language instruction: the Pennsylvania Foreign Language Project*. Philadelphia: The Center for Curriculum Development, 1970.

8 *On defining a response: a crucial problem in the analysis of verbal behavior*

STANLEY M. SAPON

In fields allied with problems of training and education, there is probably no term that has been used with a higher frequency – and with a greater range of meanings – than the term 'response.' If we limit our concerns to the fields of linguistics, psychology and language pedagogy we are still immersed in ambiguities that derive from a multiplicity of meanings. And a further complication is added by the fact that the term 'response' is also a non-technical part of the lexicon of everyday life.

What makes the definition of the 'response' crucial to any work in the area of verbal behavior is the fact that the term response has come to refer to a basic, elemental unit of behavior. The response is that which is recorded, and it is the response that is analyzed, evaluated, and scored. In foreign language teaching settings we hear of teachers' concerns with the accuracy of a student's responses, the number of correct responses, and the fluency of a student's responses. In other settings we hear of the latency of a response, the strength of a response, and the rate of responding.

In some of the instances given above, the term is used with some precision of meaning; in others, it appears to have received little or no special attention, being taken almost as a given.

A further, final stir to the mix is provided by the recent use of the hyphen to link two fields, such as psychology and linguistics, exposing us to the danger of two specialists talking to each other, each using what sounds like the same term, but which means different things to each specialist. Or worse still, slightly different things to each specialist.

The aim of this paper is to discuss some of the implications of varying uses of the term, and to explore, in critical fashion, the consequences,

both for science and pedagogy, that follow upon several common inter-
pretations of the notion of the *response*.

Let us begin with the problem as it appears in the field of psychology
itself. To the Pavlovian psychologist, the term response bears a close
resemblance to the ordinary everyday sense of the term – it means an
answer to some evoking or provoking event. In the language of the textbook, an organism makes a response to a stimulus. Or, in somewhat
different order, a stimulus evokes a response. The model of behavior
that this clearly implies, envisions an 'inventory of responses' within
the organism, pre-programmed, as it were, to appear when 'called
forth' by the appropriate stimulus. The model makes theoretical sense
and receives empirical support when it is applied to reflex behavior.
Knees jerk in response to specific percussions, pupils contract in
response to light, etc. Pavlov's great demonstration of the pairing of
unconditioned stimulus with neutral stimuli to yield a conditioned
stimulus leaves us with a conditioned response, but the response is still
the same old reflex answer to a new question. Although our primary
concern here is with *verbal* behavior, it is still fully appropriate to point
to the dangers of adopting a 'question and answer' model when dealing
with behaviors that are clearly out of the range of the built-in, reflex,
sort. Suffice it to say that the images of automaticity of behavior that it
conjures up support a mechanical view of human behavior that is non-
productive with regard to academic ambitions.

What is of greater and more immediate concern to us here is the
effect of this model on the analysis of verbal behavior. Let us think back
a moment to the earlier reference to the notion of a stimulus evoking a
response. Responses that are evoked are responses that are conceived to
lie within the organism, to pre-exist, as it were, in some tenuous,
unstructured, form, waiting to be called forth and be observed.

Although the transformationist philosophers of language inveigh
mightily against 'S–R Theory,' we find the basic framework of Pavlovian
conditioning to be much in accord with their assumptions – and
conclusions. These philosophers see 'Language' as an entity whose
awesome complexity must be explained in terms of some built-in,
genetically pre-ordained structure that makes it possible for man to
speak in what subsequent linguistic analysis reveals to be a systematic
and formally predictable fashion. There is really no difference between
the predeterminism of a Pavlovian inventory of responses with which an
organism is born and the recourse to 'the innate genetic knowledge

which the human child brings to language learning.'[1] Indeed, it is postulated that only through the intervention of this kind of meta-behavioral pre-programming, that rises above differences in specific language, can man accomplish the 'fantastic feat [of learning] that enormously extensive and complicated system which is a natural language.'[2]

What makes this system appear to be so complex? In the first place, I think, we can acknowledge this characterization as a result of what happens when specialists in the *description* of one phase of behavior come naively unprepared to the problems of the *prediction* of this same behavior. A 'horticultural linguist,' that is, one whose efforts lead to endless branches on sentence-trees, is understandably stymied at the prospect of predicting which way – specifically – a sentence will go from a given point.

That is, if we take as our only data the formal properties of an utterance, then the only predictions we can make are predictions of form, and not of substance. Given a fragment of an utterance such as 'What I really want to do is —,' a linguist can make a prediction that the next fragment of the utterance will belong to a given form class. He is utterly unprepared to specify which member of the form class called 'verbs' is likely to appear. Does the speaker want to go, stay, eat, sleep, laugh, cry, or punch his interviewer in the nose? The inability to predict which verb is likely to come next has been the source of widespread human frustration for millenia, but one school of linguists has concocted a soothing unguent for the pain of this impotence. Its principal ingredient is the word 'trivial,' which is used to describe the specific predictions which ordinary, unenlightened people are wont to consider crucial. I, for one, look with compassion upon the craftsman who does not know how to produce estimable work and settles instead for esteeming the kind of work he can do. I react in similar fashion to the linguist who, unable to draw the fine lines of specifics, points with pride to his broad sketches of form classes. I am less compassionate if this same fellow attempts to enhance his limited results by demeaning and dismissing as 'trivial' and 'uninteresting' efforts of a more exacting nature. And I remain unimpressed by the ability to predict that the last fragment of an utterance will be a member of a given class of verbs. No amount of sophistry can obscure the functionally critical nature of the question 'Which verb?'

[1] Postal (1964), p. 265. [2] *Ibid.* p. 265.

But perhaps the most fundamental reason for taking recourse to the 'hidden mysteries that lie within the organism' is the reluctance to accept the full flowering of a man's verbal behavior as the product of *learning*. And, of course, a long history of pedagogical inefficiency, yielding limited, and frequently unpredictable, success in language instruction, ultimately supports the conclusion that what is sought after may be truly 'unteachable.' This is a much more charitable interpretation than that which springs from the observation that human children, in the main, learn to speak. The fact that we cannot duplicate the phenomenon in a classroom suggests that there are major deficiencies in our instructional procedures which derive, ultimately, from inadequacies and inaccuracies in our analysis of the behaviors that we want to establish. This approach, while damaging to the ego, at least serves as a spur to further scientific work. To declare that what we have not been able to do is un-doable, and represents no less than God's Will in shaping our nervous system, is a statement worthy of a theologian, not a scientist. (Parenthetically, I can defend myself from charges of wild hyperbole by pointing to the recent spawning of 'neuro-linguistics' and 'bio-linguistics.' Theo-linguistics cannot be far behind!)

Quite current are statements to the effect that 'there is something special and unique in human beings that makes it possible for humans alone to perform in the special way we call "verbal."' Equally frequent are attempts to account for the wide range of variability of performance on the basis of undetectable, but assumed, differences in genetic structure. Such approaches do nothing more than beg the question and take us farther from the scientific objectives of prediction and control over the phenomena that we study.

One of the simplest ways of exploring the implications of the basic concepts of 'response' is to look at a number of issues phrased as unadorned, direct, questions:

(1) What do people *do*, when we say they are engaging in verbal behavior?
(2) What must they *learn* as antecedents to their final, full-fledged performance?
(3) What do we consider to be our primary data?
(4) What shall we take as our smallest unit of analysis?

The description of 'what people *do*' is frequently confounded by *a priori* descriptions of what they must *learn* in order to perform fully.

In language learning settings, it is not unusual to come upon hierarchies of what must be learned, structured in this way:

The student must

(1) first learn to pronounce *sounds*.
(2) learn to assemble the sounds to produce *words*.
(3) learn to assemble words to produce *sentences*.

A slightly different sequence sometimes offers for step (3) learning to 'generate' utterances, followed – or preceded by – the 'internalization of a set of grammatical rules' that are either derived by the learner himself or offered to him by a teacher. This listing represents not only a common strategic approach to the establishment of novel verbal behaviors, but appears to order, along some continuum of esteemed values, the assumed components of verbal behavior. This 'sorting out' of components produces a kind of crude set of definitions of what constitutes a response, giving the investigator the option of choosing the hierarchical 'level' at which he chooses to work.

A closer examination of the elements of the hierarchical strategy, however, reveals that there are unnamed elements contained in what appears to be a simple progression from *sounds* to *words* to *sentences*. These elements appear in the non-italicized parts of the list, which we will now underscore. I am referring to the notions of *learning* to *pronounce* sounds, the *assembling*, or *putting together of sounds to produce words*, and the *ordering*, *arranging* and/or *assembling of words* to *produce sentences*. These are, of course, not parts, but processes. And it is precisely at this point that linguistics, conventional or modern, finds itself in trouble, particularly when, through the medium of 'applied linguistics,' it is invited to offer solutions to the problems confronted by the language teacher. For the unique strength of linguistics began when it turned its back on mystical speculations about what really went on inside the human skull and concentrated its efforts on systematic description of what was *heard* when people speak.

Linguistics, as a discipline, acquired scientific stature primarily because it rejected the metaphysical inquiries into 'the true nature of language' that characterized its historical antecedents, and offered instead what appeared to be descriptions and analyses based on the observable primary data of human speech.

This very concern with the description and classification of speech which is a source of major strength when talking about parts is, at the

79

same time, a source of serious weakness when the discussion turns to processes. The principal reason for this lies in the common reliance upon the *speaker* as the primary source of data. It is the performance of the *speaker* that is transcribed and subjected to many varieties of analysis. The performance of the *listener* is a secondary rather than primary concern of the analyst, and when a listener is indeed called into some analytical scheme he appears as a hypothetical listener (or worse still, hypothetically typical listener) whose rôle is to judge the 'grammaticality' of a sentence or the existence of a 'minimal pair.' The notion of 'parts' and 'wholes' leads us to see the *sentence* as the unity that should be viewed as the 'whole response.' For the linguist, the sentence, as produced by the speaker, provides the data – the raw material, as it were – which is subjected to fragmentation. And it is these fragments of the speaker's production which are subjected to analysis, and which yield, for the linguist, discrete parts.

The performance of the listener, however, *qua* listener, does *not* present to the observer the kinds of performance that can be fragmented according to the analytical scheme applied to the performance of the speaker. The listener who displays his 'understanding' by following my directions to 'Bring me the third book from the left on the top shelf' certainly does not display any 'parts' of a sentence. He does display a good deal of movement, but none of this movement is transcribable in linguistic terms. It is only when he begins to talk that the listener acquires linguistic reality and existence.

What this means, in essence is that from the point of view of linguistic analysis, *responses* are made only by *speakers*. This leaves us in the odd position of describing, analyzing and predicting the performance of agents in a communication system on the basis of the *formal* properties of *one-half of the system!*

The amount of data that is actually rejected is not one-half but two-thirds. The situation can be visualized in terms of observing a man talking on the telephone, and our task it to predict what he is going to say following each pause. In a situation such as this we find we are lacking *two* elements vital to our predictions: what precedes each of his utterances (i.e. what he hears before he speaks) and what consequences follow after he speaks. All we can observe and transcribe is what happens in-between, and our predictive power functions only after the man has begun to speak. And again, this predictive power is limited – we can only predict probable sequences of 'form classes,' and not specific members thereof.

I have insisted on singling out for critical scrutiny the notion of 'form class' because its use has far-reaching implications that cross a number of disciplines. Analyses that refer to 'classes of responses' represent a kind of answer to the questions 'how do we handle massive quantities of data?' and 'What shall we take as our smallest unit of analysis?' The answer is, in effect, that we are always faced with too much data – the quantities are overwhelming and unmanageable. Before we can understand what is happening, we must reduce the number of pieces of data to manageable proportions. And we can most easily reduce this number by sorting and lumping the 'raw' data into 'classes.' One cannot argue seriously with an approach that has rendered service for a long time. But one can, and should, be concerned about how seriously the investigator takes his classifications once made. Overlooked too often is the caveat: 'Classes' are not properties of the organism we are studying. They are properties of the behavior of the observer.

It is one thing, for example, to exploit the utility of the notion of a phoneme as a *class* of sounds that function in a given way. It is something very different to forget that no organism can produce a 'class of sounds,' and to talk seriously about 'teaching a student to produce the phonemes of a language.'

One of the most damaging effects of building our thinking around notions of 'response classes' derives from the fact that such an approach serves to minimize, if not obliterate, the differences between members of the class, and leads to the tacit assumption that all items that are taken as members of the same class may be considered to be *functionally* equivalent – which might be a safe procedure if it were not for the fact that the multiplicity of 'functions' has itself been reduced to a convenient number of 'function classes!'

The notion of 'function' in the domain of linguistics has not only been restricted to the performance of the speaker, but it has also become limited to considerations of function *within the sentence*. The ultimate in functional effectiveness is seen in the Well Formed Formula, regardless of broader consequences of social survival. It is not difficult to think of a Well Formed Sentence that would earn the speaker painful and undesirable consequences administered by a Well Formed Female!

A discipline that has conceived the notion of function in terms of individual and social consequences is that of the experimental analysis of behavior. Developed and refined in laboratory settings with infrahuman organisms, its principles have been extended to the general area of human behavior, including the area defined as verbal behavior. The basic principle of its analytical framework is found in the observation that behavior is controlled by its consequences, and is represented on the tactical level by what has been called the three-term contingency model.[1] The three terms referred to are the discriminative stimulus, the response, and the consequences to the organism of that response. Unlike Pavlovian conditioning of reflexes, which offers a two-term model of a stimulus and the response to that stimulus, the three-term model permits the exercise of fine control over two-thirds of a behavioral event. That is, in the presence of a given stimulus setting (1), the emission of some performance (2), is invariably followed by some measure of environmental change for the organism (3). There are some environmental changes that increase the probability of the same performance being emitted again in the presence of the same, or similar, stimulus settings, and there are some changes, or consequences, that decrease the probability of the same performance recurring in a given setting. The predictive and controlling power that the third term adds is impressive, and we have seen the exploitation of this power in the form of programmed instruction. But we are still left with the term *response*, and the problems of defining it in the context of verbal behavior. Within the framework of behavior analysis, two properties of the 'response' appear as major concerns. One is the topography, or 'shape' of the behavior, and the other is the rate at which it is emitted.

The origins of the discipline in the laboratory, as well as the kinds of behavior selected for study and the organisms serving as experimental subjects, combine to provide a kind of historical handicap to the most productive analysis of verbal behavior. In the laboratory setting, with a rat, for example, the response is defined in terms of the muscle movements of the animal that are appropriate and sufficient to move a lever to the point of switch closure. The consequence that supports this behavior in a water-deprived animal is the appearance of a quantity of water. In this setting, then, *function* is seen as that behavior which results in the appearance of water. The *topography* of the response, i.e. the shape or form of the muscle movements that displace the lever to the point of switch closure, is ultimately determined by the mechanical properties of the lever. Since the lever is a fairly constant and reliable device, without moods or whims that depend on its immediate history prior to the arrival of the rat in the box, it regularly 'demands' only that the lever be

[1] Skinner (1953), pp. 108–10.

moved vertically through, say, a distance of 4 mm. with a force of 20 grams. The lever does not care whether it is moved with the right paw, the left paw, the nose, or even the tail. Since the apparatus does not discriminate subtle differences in topography, subtle differences in topography are not ordinarily a major part of the data on the behavior of the organism.

If the apparatus does not reveal – or call for – fine shades of difference in the topography of the behavior, neither does it reflect fine shades of difference in the field of the consequences. One functional lever-press, as defined by the operandum, is followed by one measured predetermined and invariable dose of water. We do not ordinarily see the dispensing of water in quantities related to the topography of the lever-press, e.g. a press with greater force yielding a larger quantity of water, or a corresponding relationship between the amplitude of the muscle movement and the latency of the appearance of the water.

What we have, in sum, is a binary state operandum, and a binary state reinforcement condition – a situation in which the variable most conveniently available for exploration is the frequency of the lever-presses across time, i.e. *rate*. Rate, as a measure of change in behavior, is a powerfully sensitive indicator of subtle differences in schedules of reinforcement, and rate has emerged as the variable of central importance in behavior analysis.

The appearance of a cumulative record – a measure of rate – is a consistent feature of reports on research in behavior analysis and the modification of behavior. There is, however, a singular inappropriateness in the extension of this kind of analysis to the study of verbal behavior. Rate is derived from a count of items that occur in a given time period. In the case of the animal in the experimental space, it is relatively easy to decide which items to count – lever presses – i.e. instances of the behavior we are studying. As we said before, differences in topography have been declared *a priori*, by both the investigator and the apparatus, to be of minor consequence. In essence, the count of lever presses as items declares that for the purposes of the measurement of rate, *all lever presses are considered to be functionally the same.* When we watch the same procedure applied to verbal behavior, the crucial question arises: 'What shall we consider our countable items?' It is at this crucial point that the fine-grain potential of a broadly functional analytical system becomes threatened. Can *sentences* be considered functionally the same? Can *words* be considered as functionally equivalent countable items? Can *grammatical classes* (borrowed from a form-centered discipline, whose primary data is the performance of the speaker) be considered functionally as 'sames?' Affirmative answers to these questions are indeed apparent in the literature of verbal behavior, and the result is the loss of the specificity of prediction and control that we are seeking. We are back to statements about 'increasing the number of adjectives emitted by a child.'

What seems to be perhaps the primary problem that appears throughout the various disciplines that concern themselves with human verbal behavior, is a hasty zeal to deal with 'large-scale events' and 'high-level behaviors,' coupled with a reluctance to work with the fine-grain bits of behavior at an atomic level.

Phonetics, for example, is frequently seen as being either pre-linguistic or at best, a very primitive, almost mechanical part of linguistic concerns. Phonetics also provides an overwhelming quantity of data. Granted, it represents what people – collections of persons – do with their chest and larynx and mouth, etc. All these movements of muscles, and the sounds they produce, are indeed the simple 'raw data' of human verbal behavior. But these data appear to be too raw for many people's tastes. So the raw data are rendered more manageable by moving 'up' to the phonemic level, where the number of classes is smaller, and provides access to still 'higher' levels. Which is, of course, another way of saying that we move still farther away from the goals of specificity of prediction and control!

I have asked more questions than I have answered, but the expectations of this paper were primarily to stir sleeping assumptions and provoke a more searching examination of the silent principles that underlie a good deal of contemporary work in several fields. If much of what I have said appears to be negatively oriented, I want to balance the account by concluding with a brief, but strongly positive, statement.

Directly observable verbal behavior is fundamentally nothing more or less than the resultant effects (acoustic/visual) that follow the complex movements of muscles. Although this may appear to be a *reductio ad absurdum*, it is actually an explicative reduction of a complex to its fundamental elements. The fact is that any undertaking to establish, modify, or otherwise control the verbal behavior of a human being fundamentally and inescapably revolves around these muscle movements.

On defining a response: a crucial problem in verbal behavior

A football coach may explain his interest in teaching his novices the strategies and tactics of effective playing. But the strategies and tactics of the team are evaluated on the basis of the team's *performance* – a performance represented by the observable behavior of each player, seen in terms of his body movements. If we look at a football player whose muscle movements do *not* lead to his throwing a pass that a team-mate can catch, it is pointless to discuss and evaluate his 'understanding of the game,' or his 'basic knowledge of strategy.' The real concern of the coach is with the establishment in each player of a repertoire of behaviors that leads to 'doing the right thing at the right time,' with the appropriate parts of the body.

When a foreigner says 'I have two brother' our task, and the measure of our success at it, is the changing of the speaker's muscle movements so that they yield 'I have two brothers.' Expressing concern with changing the speaker's grasp of phonological patterns or morphological structure represents a recourse to an internal grammar machine. This may indeed satisfy *post facto* curiosities, but this 'grammar machine,' intuitive and internal, resists completely any attempts to tinker with it. And since the only 'evidence' we have of its existence is the observed behavior, it must be this observed behavior that defines the responses we are obliged to deal with.

With regard to verbal behavior, it does not matter whether the investigator or teacher has declared that he is interested in 'higher levels' of 'language,' or that his concerns are with morphology or syntax. Regardless of the 'level' of his analytical or pedagogical interest, the ultimate measure of the success or failure is the specificity and appropriateness of the muscle movements of his subject. In this area, as in any other field of science, successful prediction and control of large-scale events depend on the adequate identification and fine-grained analysis of the primary and elemental components of the phenomena that concern it.

BIBLIOGRAPHY

Postal, Paul. 'Underlying and superficial linguistic structure.' *Harvard Educational Review*, **34** (1964), 246–66.
Skinner, B. F. *Science and human behavior*. New York: Macmillan, 1953.

9 Language learning strategies for the adult

D. A. REIBEL

This paper takes as its point of departure the suggestion (Corder, 1967) that the linguistic performance of the adult language learner is evidence of his possession of a strategy or built-in language learning syllabus, one which might be different from the syllabus imposed on him by the language course designer. The question then naturally arises whether this syllabus is the same for the adult as for the child. That the child has such a syllabus seems now to be beyond question (Smith and Miller, 1966). A language learning theory that ascribes the same language learning potential to the adult as to the child has been suggested before, e.g. by Sweet (1899), Jespersen (1904), and by Palmer (1922). But these typical language learning reformers felt it necessary for various reasons to superimpose on this innate language learning competence various principles of course design that determined in advance the order in which the adult learner would acquire the lexical and structural elements of the foreign language. At the same time, Palmer (1921) and Palmer and Redman (1932) recognized that while it might be correct to credit adult learners with the same innate language learning competence as the child, not all adult learners applied their competence in the same way, or even at all, and it was such differences in language learning performance that accounted for the wide variation in degree and kind of foreign language ability that is seen in adults, as opposed to children. But while the general trend in the last twenty-five or thirty years has been to deny even the possibility that the adult could in any sense learn a foreign language in the same way in which he learned his first, the question of whether or not he possesses a language learning competence like that of the child still remains to be formulated into a testable hypothesis. I should therefore like during the rest of the discussion to keep in mind not only the difficulties that stand, or can be made to stand, in the way of the adult learner, but also the fact that many adults do acquire rather remarkable skill in using foreign languages. In fact, there is a surprising number of quasi-native speakers to be found; naturally, one is not so aware of them as there are none of the usual differentia that mark them off from the population of native speakers.

One attempt to explain the differences in language learning perform-ance between adults and children takes as its starting point the observa-tion that many of the features of the learner's already known language get incorporated into the foreign language system the learner constructs for himself (Fries, 1945). While the child, as a tabula rasa, needs to consider only the primary linguistic data of one language, the adult learner has the idiosyncratic features of his first language as part of his intellectual make-up, and cannot extricate them from the stimulus system to which they function as responses. Hence interference pheno-mena arise inevitably. Such an account is bound to leave a taste of dissatisfaction in the mouths of those linguists and psychologists who no longer hold strict structuralist or behaviourist views, but what such modern linguists have done is simply to revise the theory of language learning so as to make it conform to more current views, while not abandoning the initial assumption that the adult is bound to be a different kind of learner from the child, from the point of view of his innate learning capability (McNeill, 1965; Lenneberg, 1967; Lakoff, 1969).

As long as interference phenomena are treated as the mechanical result of the learner's language learning strategy, which inexorably incorporates into the grammar of L_2 linguistic features of L_1, there is no difficulty in collecting data to support that hypothesis. The rest of this paper is devoted to the argument that an important distinction has been missed, however, by including under one schema all that the adult learner does, and that it is essential to distinguish at least two components in the language learning strategy of the adult.

Consider the distinction made by Chomsky (1965) between 'compe-tence' and 'performance'. He is of course referring to the linguistic knowledge, on the one hand, and the linguistic behaviour, on the other, of the 'idealized speaker hearer'. The first underlies, but does not fully account for, the second. While competence is necessary, it is not suffi-cient, to account for all the performance features that are the result of the interaction of very complex and overlapping systems of belief, as well as the physiological and neurological mechanisms of speech.

88

Let us extend this distinction into the field of learning as well. Thus it is useful to think of underlying learning principles, known in advance by the learner before he ever undertakes a learning task, and the procedures by which he implements these principles in a particular situation, or with a particular kind of primary data or input. Together, these principles and procedures constitute his learning strategy. In Aristotle's terminology, the learning principles are the formal cause, the procedures the efficient cause of learning. This is exactly analogous with Chomsky's distinction between competence – the formal cause – and performance – the efficient cause – of language behaviour. We will thus view the language learning process as composed of two parts: a language learning *competence*, and the actual language learning *performance*.

Of course, it is an open question what the nature of the principles of language learning are that constitute this language learning competence. Trying to specify them amounts to trying to say just what formal features or criteria of analysis would have to be built into a language learning device that replicated the language learning competence of the human being. First of all, the device would have to have some notion of phonetic representation. This feature is the analogue of the perceptual characteristic of the human learner that enables him to identify speech-sounds as such, to the exclusion of other auditory inputs. Secondly, we assume a segmentation criterion, which cuts up the linear array of speech into the phonetic, lexical, and phrasal elements that constitute the surface structure of the language act. This criterion is what allows the device to arrive at segments that match those of the grammar of the input language. In the meantime, a global semantic representation is assigned to the whole segmented phonetic representation; portions of the total semantic representation are then assigned to segments or segment-sequences of the phonetic representation. These phonetic–semantic units are then stored in such a way that access to them is possible given either the phonetic or semantic portion. At this point, we do not assume that the device has any information about the actual syntactic operations that can assemble the lexical entries into the original correct surface structure sequences. This is consonant with the claim of McNeill (1965; 1966) that in his first utterances, the child produces strings that honour the basic syntactic relations such as subject–predicate, but lack the correct surface structure form of adult utterances. In other words, the device, while segmenting the phonetic input into elemental parts and storing them, will not reassemble them correctly to match the original inputs until the intermediate (transformational) rules that distort the underlying basic structures have been learned. This is just what we find when we trace the gradual introduction into the child's speech of the features of adult speech that are the result of transformations that insert surface morphemic material, such as infinitival 'to', inflections, etc., which delete superfluous elements, and which rearrange, permute, and restructure the elements of the basic structure of the sentence.

At this point we must assume that the device is provided with a linguistic theory. By this is meant simply that the device is capable of accepting only those analyses of the data that are formulated in terms of certain constraints on the form of grammars (Chomsky, 1957). Of course, we do not know what the exact form of this theory is, but it seems inescapable that one must be present. The behaviourist–structuralist hypothesis about the nature of linguistic behaviour can be interpreted to mean that, first of all, whatever the general principles of learning, they must be applicable to language, and secondly, that whatever regularities the linguist detects in the data the procedures that he uses to arrive at his analysis are just those one would want the learning device to possess, so that it too could arrive at productive hypotheses about the linguistic form that lies behind the linguistic input. What modern linguistics has done is simply to assert that the content of this linguistic theory is much richer and more complex, hence more restrictive, than was imagined by the structuralist. What the nativist does is simply to ascribe knowledge of this theory to the learner – surely not an unreasonable thing to do if the investigation of this theory is to have any ontological, empirical, or methodological justification. The theory is indirectly confirmed by the possibility of finding that the grammars of diverse natural languages conform to the general principles of language design embodied in it. The theory is also confirmed if we find that in the course of language learning the child appears to use a succession of grammars that approximate more and more that used by the adult model, and if in doing so he seems to be adding the transformational rules that describe the relationship between the basic structures that he first produces, and the correct adult surface structures that he eventually ends up knowing.

Furthermore, Lenneberg (1967) has shown that linguistic maturation parallels physical maturation; the maturing child has a maturing linguistic theory which becomes more complex and rich with time, enabling the child to learn more and more complex structure only with the onset of certain 'maturational milestones'. The abstract device that reflects the learning capability of the child thus contains an evolving linguistic theory as well.

The claim that the child first produces sentences that honour only the basic grammatical relations while ignoring the structure superimposed on them by the transformational rules that are to be learned later, has an essential importance that should not be overlooked. Pragmatically, this knowledge provides the first provisional grammar. Such an initial step is necessary if cognition is ever to be translated into language acts. The output of the provisional grammar is available at all times for comparison with sentences of the model language. Discrepancies between the output of the provisional or interim grammar and the sentences of the model language provide the information on the basis of which the device proceeds to revise the interim grammar. This of course has consequences for certain experimental designs. If the child could detect only those features of input sentences that he himself can produce, that is, if the only structure he imposes on input sentences in perceiving them is the structure that his provisional grammar can handle at the moment, it would be impossible for him to add anything to the provisional grammar, since all phonetic and structural features of the adult sentences that impinge on him that were not allowed for in the provisional grammar would be treated as so much noise (Shipley, Gleitman, and Smith, 1969).[1]

Translated into flesh and blood, or hardware (Aristotle's material cause), we must consider the formal properties of such an abstract device as just those that we would want to be present – in some isomorphic way – in the actual device. Viewed in another way, we could imagine the actual device as a machine which is literally capable of carrying out the operations implied by the abstract device; the latter provides the criteria

[1] A corollary of this is that the adult who notices no difference between the output of his provisional (inaccurate and incomplete) grammar of L_2 and what the native speaker is saying to him will not then proceed to correct his interim grammar. But it is important to avoid seeing such a state of affairs as mechanically or deterministically defining the limits of second language learning, as attempts to account for interference phenomena sometimes do. For we must ask why the adult stops perceiving these differences, and then go on to ask whether he might not be able to revise his provisional grammar in the right direction if he did or could be made to perceive them. What is it that decides, in the case of a particular second language learner, whether he will or will not notice such features? The difficulty with any theory that ascribes a deterministic influence to previously learned linguistic rules is that it will not account for how the adult achieves the success that he does.

on the basis of which the actual device decides whether it has carried out the procedures implied by these criteria correctly or not.

Further, we note that there are characteristics of the human learner that lead him to be selective about the learning of competing systems. One interpretation of the findings in the field of sociolinguistics is that the learner seems to select from the various linguistic systems to which he is exposed the one used by a person who matches his socio-economic status (Labov, 1966). In other words, the primary linguistic data capable of functioning as a real input to the language learning competence of the learner is that produced by the speaker capable of functioning as a model to the learner. Bandura and Walters (1963) have shown the importance of the role of the model in imitative learning in a wide variety of situations, and it takes no stretch of the imagination to extend their findings into the learning of language. In particular, the model is the source of the primary data that are the input to the learning function. A complex interaction of factors, including reward-consequences to the model, affect the salience of the primary data, partially determining the degree to which the data, presented by observation and instruction, will be acquired and used. This model–learner relationship has been demonstrated in a large number of studies by Lambert (e.g. Lambert, 1963; Lambert, Havelka and Crosby, 1958) to determine degrees of attainment, and the nature of the learned second language system.

We see then that there is the logical possibility, supported by experimental evidence, that there is some innate language learning competence, which, applied in the right way, leads to linguistic competence that underlies linguistic performance. Together, the innate learning principles and their application constitute the learner's language learning strategy. We thus have the possibility of explaining the adult's language learning performance in terms of a strategy which he adopts, and we seek to explain differences between adult learners, not in terms of differences in the innate learning abilities, but rather in terms of the way in which they are applied. The adult who accepts the fluent native speaker as a suitable model, and uses his gradually increasing proficiency in the foreign language within the bounds of his expressive capabilities will not import into his foreign language speech features of his native language, *unless* he is forced or allowed to do so by factors imposed internally or externally on his expressive needs.

It has been argued by McNeill (1965) that whereas the child starts from deep structures, and proceeds to infer the transformations that lead to the correct surface structures, the adult approaches the learning of a new language from the surface structures, and then infers the transformations that lead to new deep structures, just the reverse of the child's procedure. There seem to be a number of logical difficulties with this claim, and it is hard to know what an empirical verification of it would be. First, to the extent that deep structures represent the cognitive or semantic portion of the utterance, the adult already knows how to construct them and so has no need to infer a new system of deep structures for the new language. Secondly, whereas we have pretty good evidence for what the child does – and it seems to be what McNeill says it is – we have very little information about what the adult actually does. To claim that the adult can infer new deep structures from new surface structures credits him with an auxiliary language learning skill that he possesses as an adult but not as a child, but does not explain why he should use the new one if the old one is available, or even why it should be there at all.

McNeill's second argument is that 'Once language is acquired, the distinction between the universal and the idiosyncratic aspects of language is inevitably lost' (1965, p. 19). Again, there seems to be a logical difficulty here. If the distinction between the two is *inevitably* lost, how is it ever possible for the adult to sort them out? It is not at all hard to show that adults can learn new rules in a new language where there is conflict between the new and the old, even in the case of adult learners who do poorly with the new language. Even if the adult could adopt a strategy that was like that of the child's, i.e. start from deep structures and then learn the transformations, as McNeill goes on to suggest, it is hard to see on McNeill's interpretation how the adult learner could apply the general linguistic principle that enabled him to learn the first rule in the old language to the learning of the new rule in the new language without contaminating the latter with the former, given the validity of McNeill's statement.

Yet this is just what McNeill says later on (1965, p. 20): 'In order to formulate the transformations of the second language, a foreign speaker must meet the same general condition that young children meet. They must have in mind the deep structure of a sentence as they are given the surface structure.' But if McNeill means by the term deep structure the linguistic formulation of the cognitive and semantic content of a sentence, then of course it is relatively easy to supply this in the form of explanations, translations, and all the usual tools that the language teacher uses to let his pupils know what the sentences he is teaching them mean. It is not necessary to do as McNeill argues one might do: 'provide them with sentences constructed on the same pattern as sentences produced by very young children learning that same language' (1965, p. 21). That is, if it is desirable for adults to start from deep structures, then there is still the question, as there so often is when the desirability of having certain kinds of features in a language learning programme is pointed out, whether it is necessary to have a *special procedure* for ensuring that the programme has that feature (Reibel, 1969).

Now what did the adult do who learned a foreign language well or nearly perfectly? I would like to suggest the nature of research that might bear on this question, although to my knowledge none of this particular type has been done. While research into child language learning is being carried out by longitudinal studies, it seems curious that up to now research on adult language learning has typically proceeded by means of synchronic studies of interference phenomena. This has of course an explanation: the belief that the knowledge of one language will form part of the adult's learning strategy in learning a second. It only remains then to find out which features of L_1 will be transferred to L_2. Such research is not without interest, but it leaves unanswered a whole host of other questions, in particular what is the adult's strategy when, after a period of relative inarticulateness, he manages to acquire some performance skill in a foreign language, finally to end up with near or quasi-native competence. Quite a few methods of research suggest themselves, such as the study of spontaneous speech of adult learners over time to see the order in which certain features are acquired; acceptability experiments such as those of Quirk and Svartvik (1966); and the manipulation of various environmental conditions to determine their influence on speed and accuracy of learning. (They are listed here in ascending order of complexity of interpretation.)

The technique of analysis of errors could be adapted to study changes in underlying rule systems over time, as in some present work in child and infancy research. The acceptability tests mentioned might prove less valuable than at first hoped. If in clear cases of differences in performance skill two populations give the same or very similar results on such tests, then the validity of such tests is called into question. To the extent that foreign learners of English, for example, make the same judgements as native speakers, they will be said to exhibit the same competence, in the sense of Chomsky (1965). But such cases must be matched by equal or equivalent fluency and skill in English for such tests to be of interest in answering the question of adult language learning strategies.

What I have suggested in this paper is that the language learning strategy adopted by the adult has at least two components: underlying principles of learning and analysis, applicable to primary linguistic data, and eventually yielding competence in a foreign language equivalent to that of a native speaker, and allowing the same performance skills; and secondly, a method of applying these underlying learning principles, controlled by various situational and personal factors that set effective limits to language learning performance, and which may determine the nature of the resulting competence. We explain the differences among adult learners, and the difference between child and adult, by reference to the total strategy each uses; logically, there is no difficulty in imputing the same innate knowledge of underlying learning principles to both.[1]

BIBLIOGRAPHY

Bandura, A., and Walters, R. H. *Social learning and personality development.* New York: Holt, Rinehart and Winston, 1963.
Chomsky, Noam. *Syntactic structures.* The Hague: Mouton, 1957.
    Aspects of the theory of syntax. Cambridge, Mass.: M.I.T. Press, 1965.
Corder, S. P. 'The significance of the learner's errors.' *IRAL*, **5** (1967), 161–70.
Fries, C. C. *Teaching and learning English as a foreign language.* Ann Arbor, Mich.: University of Michigan Press, 1945.
Huxley, J. S. *Evolution in action.* London: Chatto and Windus, 1953.
Jespersen, Otto. *How to teach a foreign language.* London: Allen and Unwin, 1904. (Reprinted 1956.)
Labov, William. *The social stratification of English in New York City.* Washington, D.C.: Center for Applied Linguistics, 1966.
Lakoff, Robin. 'Transformational grammar and language teaching.' *Language Learning*, **19** (1969), 117–40.

[1] The insight to be gained from diachronic study of synchronic states has been succinctly expressed by Huxley (1953, p. 33): 'When we take an instantaneous snapshot, we freeze the process into a set of unreal static pictures. What we need is the equivalent of a film. We all know how a film record can be speeded up to reveal processes that are hidden from ordinary view...The same applies to our moving picture of evolution. If this is run at what seems natural speed, we see only individual lives and deaths. But when, with the aid of our scientific knowledge and imagination, we alter the time scale of our vision, new processes become apparent...Only in the longest perspective, with a hundred-thousand-fold speed-up, do over-all processes of evolution become visible – the replacement of old types by new...the narrow and winding stairway of progress.' For 'evolution', read 'language acquisition'; for 'individual lives and deaths', read 'successive interim grammars'. (This reference is due to Wang, 1969.)

Lambert, W. E. 'Behavioral evidence for contrasting forms of bilingualism.' In Zarechnak, 1963.

Lambert, W. E., Havelka, J., and Crosby, C. 'The influence of language-acquisition contexts on bilingualism.' *Journal of Abnormal and Social Psychology*, **56** (1958), 239–44.

Lenneberg, E. H. *Biological foundations of language*. New York: Wiley, 1967.

McNeill, D. 'Some thoughts on first and second language acquisition.' Cambridge, Mass.: Harvard University, Center for Cognitive Studies, 1965. 'Developmental psycholinguistics.' In Smith and Miller, *The genesis of language*, pp. 15–84.

Palmer, H. E. *The oral method of teaching languages*. Cambridge: Heffer, 1921. *The principles of language study*. London: Harrap, 1922.

Palmer, H. E., and Redman, H. V. *This language learning business*. London: Harrap, 1932.

Quirk, R., and Svartvik, J. *Investigating linguistic acceptability*. The Hague: Mouton, 1966.

Reibel, D. A. 'Language learning analysis.' *IRAL*, **7** (1969), 283–94.

Shipley, E. F., Gleitman, L. R., and Smith, C. S. 'A study in the acquisition of language: free responses to commands.' *Language*, **45** (1969), 322–42.

Smith, F., and Miller, G. A. *The genesis of language: a psycholinguistic approach*. Cambridge, Mass.: M.I.T. Press, 1966.

Sweet, H. *The practical study of languages: a guide for teachers and learners*. London: Dent, 1899.

Wang, W. S.-Y. 'Competing changes as cause of residue.' *Language*, **45** (1969), 9–25.

Zarechnak, Michael (ed.). *Report of the Twelfth Annual Round Table Meeting on Linguistics and Language Studies* (Georgetown University Monograph Series on Language and Linguistics, no. 14, 1961), Washington, D.C.: Georgetown University Press, 1963, pp. 73–80.

IO   *On some modalities of syntactic productivity and choice*[1]

RENZO TITONE

INTRODUCTION

The present research received inspiration from a theoretical essay by
Wallace L. Chafe (1967) and from an empirical investigation conducted by
J. Dubois and L. Irigaray (1966). Both place in bold relief the role played
by semantic factors in the production of grammatical sentences.

In his article on language as symbolization, Chafe outlines a system of
language which consists essentially of two components, a semological
and a phonological. Semological units are those manifested directly in
experience, while phonological units are the sound manifestations which
symbolize semological units. According to Chafe, 'In consequence of
both its evolutionary and non-evolutionary history, language exhibits an
initial organization of experience within deep semology, a set of mutations which lead to surface semology, an initial phonological symbolization, and another set of mutations which lead to a final phonological
organization manifested in sound' (1967, p. 57).

The principal question pondered by Chafe is the place of separate
semantic and syntactic components in a description of the communication process. Any consideration of this problem has been hampered by
limitations in the study of the nature of language imposed by some
linguistic theories. Fortunately, these strictures are currently being
relaxed, and such study even encouraged, so that many psycholinguistic
works on the ontogeny and acquisition of language, as well as its use in
the process of communication, are deepening an understanding of the
dynamic nature of language.

One such study has been conducted by J. Dubois and L. Irigaray
(1966), in which the authors concentrate on the production of sentences
under testing conditions with control of different variables. Their

[1] This paper has already appeared in *IRAL*, **8** (1970).

intention was to study the strategy of normal, aphasic, and schizophrenic subjects in the production of sentences in determined linguistic conditions, with particular concentration on conditions of ambiguity. Sketched in their article is a preliminary analysis of sentence production performed by normal subjects. The subjects' task consisted in the production of sentences of minimal length using words given (from two to five). Presumably kernel sentences, e.g. active, positive, were to occur, and the testing was done both orally and in written form.

The authors operated on the hypothesis that syntactic and/or semantic correlations between lexical classes would occur in varying degrees depending on the nature and function of the constitutive parts of the given utterance (p. 92). Thus what the authors call 'intrasyntagmatic constraints' will be strongest, e.g. determiner plus noun, adjective plus noun, noun plus possessive noun phrase, and it was postulated that sentences where constraints are strongest will be more difficult to generate than sentences where constraints are less rigorous. Intrasyntagmatic, intrapropositional, and interpropositional relations were studied. It was expected that a conflict would exist between the order of presentation of stimulus words, and the linear arrangement of the stimulus words in the utterances made necessary by syntactic considerations. Thus, for example, if an inanimate noun, a transitive verb, and an animate noun were given in that order as stimuli, the kernel sentence structure in the active voice would demand using the animate noun first in most cases. The subject, therefore, is confronted with a choice in word order.

Dubois and Irigaray claim three hypotheses verified (p. 100):

(1) Where lexical classes of nouns were dissimilar, the animate noun was most often used as subject of the sentence, and the inanimate as object.

(2) Where lexical classes of nouns were similar various techniques were used. If both nouns were animate, they were used as a compound subject of the verb. If the nouns were inanimate, either two sentences were produced, or the underlying second sentence became a noun phrase.

(3) Verbs were used corresponding to the noun class, usually in a transitive active form.

These correlations overruled any influence by the order of presentation of the stimulus words.

Semantic sub-classes of nouns and verbs were further identified.

In conclusion, the authors state that the study of strategies adopted by speakers permits definition and hierarchization of syntactic facts. It is felt that an experimental approach to the analysis of certain transformations can give an objective basis to the study of the psychology of syntactic production.

SCOPE AND PURPOSE OF THE PRESENT RESEARCH

The purpose of my investigation was very similar to the one proposed by Dubois and Irigaray for theirs. My intention was basically to analyze the dynamics of semantic–syntactic relations in the production of acceptable and grammatical sentences. The analysis was to be conducted with three aspects in mind: (a) the production of sentences with given strings of random words (from two to six); (b) the choice of a series of acceptable meanings, given a set of polysemic lexemes, as a function of valid syntactic context; (c) motivated choice of the active or passive voice in constructing a simple sentence given a variable number of words.

A major difference from the Dubois and Irigaray investigation was the comparative point of view. Results were to be compared in terms of three variables: (a) age, (b) culture, and (c) language mastery. To this end the *S*s were distinguished according to age level, culture, and degree of linguistic mastery, with the cultural denominator somewhat overlapping between the groups. The introduction of the comparative perspective was motivated by the desire to verify a broader generalizability of the results found by the French investigators, and at the same time to transfer the analysis of results onto the fields of first and second language learning.

So far only the first part of the research has been evaluated. It yields two sets of data: one set of results concerns what I have called 'Productivity Quotient' (PQ), indicating the average number of sentences produced by each individual on the basis of each word string; a second group of features refers to some characteristics of semantic–syntactic distribution. My report will, therefore, summarize only data related to these two points.

PROCEDURES USED

The *S*s were divided into five groups: A. Italian junior secondary school students (22; average age 13); B. Italian university graduate students (12; av. age 23); C. Italian post-doctoral students (15; av. age 27); D. American university graduate students (13; av. age 25); E. Mixed nationality students (speakers of Spanish 2, German 1, Indonesian 1, Vietnamese 1, Ethiopian–Amharic 1, Japanese 1, French–Canadian 1, Brazilian 2, Dutch 1 : 11 ; av. age 25). The inter-chronological correlation was to be found between groups A on one side and B, C on the other; the inter-cultural and inter-linguistic correlation was to be found between groups A, B, C on one side and D, E on the other, and then between E and D, respectively. The mixed nationality group (E) consisted of foreign but near-native speakers of English.

The investigation was based on written responses to three subtests. The first subtest consisted of five series of random words (from two to six). On the basis of each group of words the subject was supposed to construct all the sentences that he thought possible, (1) making sure that each sentence was acceptable and grammatical, (2) choosing freely between either simple or complex constructions, (3) adding sparingly in each sentence only those contentives and/or functives which were necessary for each construction and strictly pertinent to the meaning assigned to the sentences. The second subtest consisted of a set of eight polysemic words with which the subject was supposed to build all possible simple sentences endowed with a clear meaning and based on the meanings that could be lawfully assigned to each such word. The third subtest, aiming at testing choice of the active or passive voice, was based on five groups of stimulus-words. The subject was supposed to build a simple sentence by choosing a verb which he would freely place in the active or passive. Then, he was asked to cite one reason explaining his choice.

The time allotted to the administration of this battery of tests was 90 minutes.

PRELIMINARY AND PARTIAL RESULTS

As mentioned before, the results given here refer only to the first part of the test and even these have not yet been submitted to deeper qualitative analysis. I hope to be able to present more interesting observations after each response item has been analyzed more carefully. Here also only some of the major aspects will be dwelt on while other details can be gathered by referring to the eleven tables added in the Appendix.

Most of my results seem to confirm the hypotheses proposed by Dubois and Irigaray, while others demand more accurate verification and further analysis. Following is a summary of conclusions.

Productivity Quotient (PQ)

From the general viewpoint of the relation between number of given words and number of individual syntactic combinations, there seems to be a constancy of inverse ratio, i.e. the number of constructed sentences diminishes in proportion to the increase of the number of stimulus-words given by the experimenter, this inverse ratio being of between one-third and one-fifth. This constant characteristic of progressive limitation of combinatorial indices, while it would not be justifiable in terms of mathematical and linguistic logic, seems to have a psycholin-guistic or at least a psychological explanation in the fact that the Ss tend to find it more and more difficult and cumbersome to combine a longer string of random words than to multiply combinations of shorter strings. Perhaps limitation of time and the impression of cumbersome-ness can be invoked as factors limiting the individual's combinatory activity.

Generally speaking, adults show a higher combinatory power (e.g. young adolescents (Group A) in word string 1·1 reach a PQ of 5·5 compared with adults (Groups C, D, E) reaching a PQ of 6·7 and 8·1), and also greater resistance of high PQs vis-à-vis increase of stimulus-words (e.g. in word string 1·5 young adolescents (A), PQ 1·02, compared with adults (B, C, D, E), PQs 2·3, 2·1, 3·7, and 2·6). These two traits can be considered as genetically significant in that combinatory power can be safely related to degree of mental and linguistic development. On the other hand, combinatory power does not seem to differentiate signifi-cantly native speakers from near-native learners (of English). The PQs of the two groups D and E do not differ considerably in the two lists. (The high PQ 8·1 in word string 1·1 for Group E may be accounted for simply by motivationally contingent factors, not by higher ability for syntactic production.)

Of course, such results could easily be anticipated, but the merit of empirical verification lies in being able to determine exact measures of performance and differential characterization. It is of psychological in-terest, for example, to be able to define that adult speakers show a combinatorial ability which is more than one point higher than that of young adolescents.[1]

[1] 'One point' (1.0) refers here to our measure of the Productivity Quotient in syntactic encoding.

Characteristics of semantic–syntactic distribution

The preliminary results of the present investigation suggest a series of statements about the existence of definable interrelationships between the semantic and the syntactic axes of language in the production of meaningful sentences. Such statements can be formulated as follows:

(1) Where lexical classes of nouns are dissimilar (animate versus inanimate), the animate noun is regularly used as subject of the sentence, and the inanimate as object (direct or indirect object). The two words 'mother' (*madre*) and 'boy' (*ragazzo*) retain the highest relative frequency of occurrence in subject position regardless of difference in age and/or culture (cf. Tables 2a, 2b, 3a, 3b). The order of stimulus presentation was altogether overruled by semantic choice: despite the presentation of 'house' (*casa*) in first position in the given string (1·1) and of 'boy' (*ragazzo*) in second position in a three-word string (1·2), the inanimate noun never received subject function and the animate noun was always and only placed as subject of the sentences produced.

(2) Where lexical classes of nouns are similar and both nouns are inanimate, either two sentences are produced, or the underlying second sentence becomes a noun phrase, or again the first word presented as a stimulus in the given string is used as subject. The third solution is commonly adopted by the junior *S*s who place the first word (*luce*, 'light') in the given string in subject position (73·5%). The suggestive influence of the stimulus takes over the burden of decision. The choice made by the adults in all four remaining groups is quite different: they all agree in making a reasoned decision based apparently on a logical dependence between 'light' and 'lamp', the latter being the source of light and therefore, grammatically, the subject of the sentences produced ('lamp' has the highest frequencies in subject position with Groups B, C, D, and E).

(3) Inanimate nouns with 'space' as a semantic component are most frequently placed in the locative. For example, 'house' (*casa*) is mainly found in syntagmatic constructions signifying 'site' or 'location', as in forms like 'in the house', 'to his house' (*a casa*); the same ought to be said for 'school' (*scuola*), 'room' (*stanza*), 'table' (*tavolo*); and 'paper' (*foglio*) acquires a locative value by being usually connected with 'write' and 'pen' (*scrivere, penna*), as in 'He writes *on the paper* with the blue pen' (*Scrive sul foglio con la penna blu*). It must be mentioned parenthetically, however, that the *S*s of Group D (native Americans) used

also an inanimate space noun, 'house', in subject position rather frequently (34·09%), although less often than the other word in the string, 'mother' (59·09%). One may wonder whether this trend of choice denotes a cultural bias whereby Americans appear to be less 'mother-dependent' and more prone to value such material goods as a 'house'. But, of course, this can be no more than just amusing speculation.

(4) The verb as a rule is chosen depending on the class of the noun acting as subject in the sentence. If the noun is animate, verbs are usually transitive active. If the noun is inanimate, the verb is frequently passive or 'middle', meaning by 'middle' a verb like *be, become, belong*, etc. The choice of the passive seems to depend on the tendency of the speaker to shift the responsibility for 'agency' from explicit inanimate nouns to implicit animate referents. This confirms one impression about a general trend underlying sentence construction, namely that syntax is closer to the serial order of thought than morphology; in other words that certain basic functions of the syntactic system correlate somewhat more closely with features of the cognitive processes, which constitute the contents ready to be verbalized. The 'syntactic subject' is somehow equated by the conscious speaker with the 'self', i.e. with an agent which is the responsible source of activity (and, in an utterance, with a generative pivot which is the starting point of a representational sequence).

This last remark brings the interpreter of an investigation such as the present one to the realization that psycholinguistic analysis of syntactic encoding involves much more than just a grammatical model to be rigorously applied to a constructed corpus, and much more than a semantic model to be added to grammar as a patchwork, but it requires an eclectic consideration of the many complex factors (psychological, linguistic, cultural, situational, experiential, etc.) which play an active and indispensable role in the actual production of a speech act (*parole*). In more comprehensive terms, one ought to say that even a simple act of syntactic encoding having real meaning in a communication situation cannot dispense with the whole of the speaker's personality as a multidimensional and unique source of the individual's learning, experience, and behavior.

SOME GENERAL CONCLUSIONS

The tentative character of some of the above conclusions does not diminish the validity and suggestiveness of the following final remarks:

(1) A definite interdependence between semantic values and syntactic functions is apparent in the normal construction of sentences.

(2) A satisfactory interpretation of the process of syntactic encoding ought to be based on an adequate consideration of the complex personality structure of the individual speaker.

(3) Generally speaking, and from an epistemological point of view, it can be proposed that the experimental approach in psycholinguistic analysis enables the linguist to go beyond the mere generative 're-writing' technique in describing transformations by affording the possibility of discovering deep psycholinguistic causes underlying grammatical transformations.

However, some scientific weaknesses are apparent both in the work of Dubois and Irigaray, and in my own investigation. Lack of a satisfactory descriptive model, from a linguistic standpoint, inadequate experimental design, insufficient empirical measurement, insufficient isolation of the stylistic variables, and an excessively generic formulation of hypotheses ought to be eliminated in future projects.[1]

BIBLIOGRAPHY

Chafe, Wallace L. 'Language as symbolization.' *Language*, **43** (1967), 57–91.
Dubois, J., and Irigaray, L. 'Approche expérimentale des problèmes intéressant la production de la phrase noyau et ses constituants immédiats.' *Langages*, **3** (Sept. 1966), 90–125.

[1] The author wishes to acknowledge his indebtedness to all those who co-operated in this research both in Italy and in the United States: Dr A. Amato (University of Rome), Dr E. Arcaini (University of Bologna), Dr G. Esposito (North Italy Public Schools), Miss M. A. Shiels and Mr Richard E. Tenney (Georgetown University).

APPENDIX

Table 1: *Productivity Quotients (PQs)*

Word strings	A TS	A PQ	B TS	B PQ	C TS	C PQ	D TS	D PQ	E TS	E PQ
1.1	112	5.5	64	5.3	101	6.7	88	6.7	65	8.1
1.2	46	2.09	38	3.1	45	3.0	75	5.7	46	5.7
1.3	46	2.09	40	3.3	41	2.7	75	5.7	45	5.6
1.4	46	2.09	32	2.6	33	2.2	58	4.4	41	5.1
1.5	28	1.02	28	2.3	32	2.1	48	3.7	23	2.6
Totals	278		202		252		344		220	Grand total 1,296 Ss 73

Notes

A, Italian junior secondary school students (*Ss* 22); B, Italian university students (*Ss* 12); C, Italian post-doctoral students (*Ss* 15); D, American university graduate students (*Ss* 13); E, Mixed nationality students (*Ss* 11); TS, Total number of Sentences; PQ, Productivity Quotient (in sentence construction)

Abbreviation code for syntactic analysis in Tables 2a–6b

S	Subject	*Poss*	Possessive
IO	Indirect Object	*Vb*	Verb
DO	Direct Object	*Ac*	Active
NP	Noun Predicate	*Pas*	Passive
A	Attribute	*Voc*	Vocative
Ad	Adverb		

Tables 2a–6b: Analysis of word strings in Table 1

TABLE 2a. *Analysis of word string 1·1 (casa, madre)*

Words	Syntactic distribution	A (%)	B (%)	C (%)
Madre	S	66.1	70.3	61.3
	DO	0.8	—	0.9
	IO	10.7	6.2	6.9
	NP	—	—	3.1
	A	—	—	—
	Poss	—	18.7	23.8
	Vb	—	—	—
	Voc	—	—	—
Casa	S	16.9	28.1	26.4
	DO	20.5	26.4	16.8
	IO	29.5	34.3	42.5
	A	—	—	—
	Poss	—	3.1	9.9
	NP	—	—	4.6
	Vb	—	—	—

TABLE 2b. *Analysis of word string 1·1 (house, mother)*

Words	Syntactic distribution	D (%)	E (%)
House	S	34.09	24.5
	DO	27.2	41.5
	IO	29.5	20.0
	NP	4.5	4.3
	A	4.5	2.1
	Poss	—	—
	Vb	1.1	1.5
Mother	S	59.09	73.8
	DO	7.9	5.8
	IO	13.63	16.9
	NP	4.5	1.5
	A	2.2	—
	Poss	10.2	2.1
	Vb	—	—
	Voc	2.2	—

TABLE 3a. *Analysis of word string 1·2 (ricompensa, ragazzo, scuola)*

Words	Syntactic distribution	A (%)	B (%)	C (%)
Ricompensa	S	8.03	3.0	18.6
	DO	50.0	23.0	46.6
	IO	6.5	4.0	8.8
	NP	—	2.0	8.8
	A	—	—	—
	Poss	—	—	—
	Vb			
	Ac	24.7	4.0	15.5
	Pas	4.3	—	—
Ragazzo	S	52.6	23.0	42.2
	DO	28.2	3.0	15.5
	IO	13.04	9.0	37.7
	NP	—	1.0	—
	Poss	—	1.0	—
Scuola	S	30.4	11.0	26.6
	DO	6.5	1.0	6.6
	IO	56.7	26.0	66.6

TABLE 3b. *Analysis of word string 1.2 (reward, boy, school)*

Words	Syntactic distribution	D (%)	E (%)
Reward	S	13.3	8.7
	DO	34.6	71.7
	IO	5.4	—
	NP	20.0	8.7
	A	4.0	4.3
	Poss	—	—
	Vb	26.6	13.4
Boy	S	46.6	60.8
	DO	22.5	4.3
	IO (to-whom)	24.0	28.2
	NP	—	6.7
	Poss	5.4	8.7
School	S	24.0	30.4
	DO	5.4	10.8
	IO	56.0	63.04
	A	13.3	2.4
	Vb	1.3	—
	Voc	1.3	—

TABLE 4a. *Analysis of word string* 1·3 *(luce, lampada, stanza, tavolo)*

Words	Syntactic distribution	A (%)	B (%)	C (%)
Luce	S	73.5	14.0	43.9
	DO	34.7	13.0	41.4
	IO	6.5	12.0	7.3
Lampada	S	43.4	22.0	53.6
	DO	8.7	2.0	7.3
	IO	13.04	3.0	4.4
	Poss	26.3	12.0	31.7
Stanza	S	4.3	2.0	9.7
	DO	17.4	4.0	9.7
	IO	67.4	18.0	46.3
	NP	—	1.0	—
	Poss	13.0	10.0	34.1
Tavolo	S	24.7	4.0	12.1
	DO	21.7	3.0	14.6
	IO	54.3	29.0	65.8
	Poss	—	—	4.4

TABLE 4b. *Analysis of word string* 1·3 *(light, lamp, room, table)*

Words	Syntactic distribution	D (%)	E (%)
Light	S	29.2	20.0
	DO	22.5	26.6
	IO	9.2	8.8
	NP	5.4	6.6
	A	17.2	15.5
	Vb	16.0	24.4
Lamp	S	33.3	28.8
	DO	19.9	28.8
	IO	33.3	28.8
	NP	4.0	11.1
	A	6.6	2.2
Room	S	5.4	11.1
	DO	13.3	22.2
	IO	73.4	57.7
	NP	1.3	2.2
	A	4.0	2.2
	Poss	1.3	—
Table	S	13.3	2.2
	DO	9.2	11.1
	IO	60.0	60.0
	NP	—	8.8
	A	13.3	11.1
	Vb	1.3	—

TABLE 5a. *Analysis of word string 1·4 (penna, bianco, foglio, scrivere, blu)*

Words	Syntactic distribution	A (%)	B (%)	C (%)
Penna	S	52.6	9.0	21.2
	DO	2.1	8.0	12.1
	IO	39.1	15.0	63.6
	Poss	2.1	—	—
Bianco	A	84.7	30.0	81.8
	NP	8.6	—	9.03
	Ad	4.3	—	6.06
	IO	—	1.0	—
Foglio	S	17.4	2.0	15.1
	DO	—	6.0	24.1
	IO	69.5	24.0	57.2
	Poss	—	1.0	—
Scrivere	Vb			
	Ac	86.9	30.0	93.9
	Pas	6.7	1.0	6.06
Blu	A	60.8	25.0	57.2
	NP	4.3	—	6.06
	Ad	23.9	5.0	21.2
	IO	2.1	1.0	6.06

TABLE 5b. *Analysis of word string 1·4 (pen, white, paper, write, blue)*

Words	Syntactic distribution	D (%)	E (%)
Pen	S	32.7	21.9
	DO	25.8	34.1
	IO	48.2	46.3
	Vb	1.7	—
White	A	98.2	87.7
	IO	—	4.8
	DO	—	4.8
	NP	—	4.8
Paper	S	8.6	7.3
	DO	18.9	17.07
	IO	67.2	70.7
Write	A	6.9	4.8
	Vb	84.4	90.2
Blue	S	1.7	—
	NP	1.7	—
	A	96.5	87.8
	DO	—	4.8
	IO	—	4.8

TABLE 6a. *Analysis of word string* 1.5 (*libro, scolaro, pagina, prendere, staccare, banco*)

Words	Syntactic distribution	A (%)	B (%)	C (%)
Libro	S	7.1	7.0	6.5
	DO	71.4	50.0	50.0
	IO	14.3	32.0	37.5
	Poss	10.7	7.0	9.3
Scolaro	S	92.1	79.0	65.6
	DO	—	—	—
	IO (to-whom)	7.1	7.0	15.6
	Poss	10.7	11.0	18.7
Pagina	S	21.4	18.0	15.6
	DO	82.1	71.0	78.1
	IO	—	4.0	9.3
Prendere	Vb			
	Ac	82.1	79.0	84.3
	Pas	17.8	14.0	12.5
Staccare	Vb			
	Ac	78.5	57.0	71.7
	Pas	14.3	7.0	15.6
	NP	3.5	21.0	6.5
Banco	S	—	—	—
	DO	3.5	7.0	6.5
	IO	96.4	71.0	84.3
	Poss	—	—	6.5

TABLE 6b. *Analysis of word string* 1·5 (*book, student, page, take, pull out, desk*)

Words	Syntactic distribution	D (%)	E (%)
Book	S	6.2	4.3
	DO	52.08	43.4
	IO	35.4	47.8
	NP	2.08	—
	A	4.1	—
	Poss	2.08	—
Student	S	77.08	86.9
	DO	2.08	—
	IO (to-whom)	12.5	4.3
	A	4.1	4.3
	Poss	8.2	—
	NP	—	4.3
Page	S	10.4	13.04
	DO	79.1	47.8
	IO	14.5	26.08
	A	2.08	4.3
Take	Vb	91.5	95.6
Pull out	IO	4.1	—
	A	8.2	4.3
	Vb	85.4	91.3
Desk	S	6.2	8.6
	DO	4.1	4.3
	IO	83.3	78.2
	A	4.1	—
	Poss	2.08	—

II The effectiveness of two learning models: the audio-lingual habit theory and the cognitive code-learning theory

THEODORE H. MUELLER

Audio-lingual language teaching has come under severe criticism by linguists and by psychologists interested in human learning. According to Carroll, 'there are today two major theories of foreign language learning. One may be called the *audio-lingual habit theory;* the other, the *cognitive code-learning theory*.'[1] He concludes: 'We need information on which of these theories is a better basis for foreign language teaching.'[2]

THE AUDIO-LINGUAL HABIT THEORY

The audio-lingual method, also called the Fundamental Skills method, views language as behavior, and is based on behaviorist psychology and structural linguistics.

Behaviorist psychology stresses repetition of the item under study, and relies on the conditioning process. It assumes that 'analogy provides a better foundation for foreign-language learning than analysis.'[3] 'Memorization and manipulation of patterns which bring out partial resemblances, or similarities of structure, beneath surface variations of vocabulary' form the psychological basis of this method.[4]

Structural linguistics, with its emphasis on speech over the written language, and its insistence that the spoken language must be mastered before the learning of the written system, forms the second foundation of the method. Structural linguists, too, consider language as a complex set of habits.[5]

[1] Carroll, in Valdman (1966), p. 101.   [2] *Ibid.* p. 102.
[3] Rivers (1964), p. 115.   [4] *Ibid.* p. 117.   [5] Ferguson, in Mead (1966).

Pattern drills are the result of these two influences, with the internalization of language habits as their objective.

THE COGNITIVE CODE-LEARNING THEORY

Gestalt psychology and transformational linguistics form the basis of this second method.

The psychological theories which Carroll mentions emphasize the following principles:

(1) The frequency with which an item is contrasted with other items is more important than frequency of repetition.
(2) The more meaningful the materials with which the student works the greater the facility in retention.
(3) Materials presented visually are more easily learned than comparable materials presented aurally.
(4) Conscious attention to critical features and understanding of them will facilitate learning.[1]

On the basis of these principles, greater importance is attached to acquiring conscious control of the patterns through study and analysis than through analogy. Greater importance is given to understanding the structure than to facility in using it.

Transformational linguists view language as an abstract system. To them it is rule-governed behavior. They insist on the innovative aspect of language, and attach no particular importance to the pre-eminence of speech over writing. The exercises developed under the influence of such linguistic principles go beyond habit formation, and insist on understanding of the language code. They aim at increasing the student's repertory of choices among the various patterns and at imparting a sensitivity to the meaning of patterns. Specifically, the presentation of the grammatical system undergoes an essential modification. The structures are presented as a related system from the top, that is, from the sentence pattern level down to the morphemic level. It is posited that, in this way, the student will be more readily induced to the language system and will internalize the rules that govern the target language. In terms of Gestalt psychology, he is taught to perceive structural relationships, called 'transposition', as opposed to transferring similar elements by the process of analogy.

If we take the word group introduced by *du, de la, des* as an example,

[1] Carroll, in Valdman (1966), pp. 104–5.

we see that the explanations given under the influence of the cognitive code-learning theory emphasize that this type of word group occurs in two different types of basic sentence patterns:

(1) A variant of the direct object sentence pattern. Its negative transform must use *de*. It is contrasted with the other variants of the same pattern and their transforms.
(2) A variant of the prepositional phrase sentence pattern. Its negative transform does not affect the preposition and the noun marker.

All structures are presented as one of only a very limited number of basic sentence patterns, each being taught with its various transforms, such as the negative, the pronominal, the interrogative transform, etc. The cognitive code-learning presentation of the *du, de la, des* group is summarized in Table 1.

TABLE 1. *Cognitive code-learning presentation of the word group with* du, de la, des

Direct object sentence pattern			
S	V	NM	DO
L'épicier	vend	de la la sa	viande maison voiture
Negative transform			
L'épicier	ne vend pas	de la sa	viande maison voiture
Prepositional phrase sentence pattern			
S	V	Prep NM	
Je	parle	de la du des	dame garçon enfants
Il	vient	du	bureau
Negative transform			
Je	ne parle pas	de la du des	dame garçon enfants
Il	ne vient pas	du	bureau

In an audio-lingual approach, *du, de la, des* is treated as a partitive noun marker of a noun phrase irrespective of its syntactical slot. It is then presented again as a combination of the preposition *de* and the definitive noun marker in a prepositional phrase which is the complement of a verb or of a noun (as in *la facture du boucher*). Under the heading of negative structures, the form *de* is introduced, without reference to specific sentence patterns. The audio-lingual approach emphasizes the forms and the patterns of the word-group. By de-emphasizing structural hierarchy it greatly multiplies the number of patterns to be learned. It relies on overlearning, so that the specific pattern is used subconsciously.

To implement the objectives of the cognitive code-learning principles, new kinds of exercises have been developed, which, in one and the same exercise, require the production of various and divergent patterns and which demand conscious attention to the pattern and to the meaning of what is to be said. They maximize the discrimination process by which the student learns to perceive the limits of the generalization, and to make the necessary distinctions. They are designed to make him generate new sentences with a minimum of cues. Examples of such exercises are set out below.

EXERCISES BASED ON THE COGNITIVE CODE-LEARNING THEORY

Exercise I

Demandez-lui s'il prend du café.
Student A: Est-ce que vous prenez du café?
Student B: Non, je ne prends pas de café.
Demandez-lui s'il prend le train.
                  s'il vient de la gare.
                  s'il apprend le français.
                  s'il veut des livres.

Exercise II

A: Vous avez parlé d'elle?　B: Parlé de qui?
A: Parlé de la veuve.　B: Non, je n'ai pas parlé de la veuve.
A: Vous vous en méfiez? B: Méfiez de quoi?
A: Méfiez de la publicité. B: Non, je ne me méfie pas de la publicité.
A: Vous en avez reçu?　B: Reçu quoi?
A: Reçu du vin. B: Non, je n'ai pas reçu de vin.

Exercise III

Demandez-lui s'il a parlé des traits de caractère français.

A: Est-ce que vous avez parlé des traits de caractère français?
B: Oui, bien sûr, j'en ai parlé. Et vous?
A: Non, je n'ai pas parlé des traits de caractère français.

Demandez-lui s'il veut du vin de Champagne.

A: Est-ce que vous voulez du vin de Champagne?
B: Oui, bien sûr, j'en veux. Et vous?
A: Non, je ne veux pas de vin de Champagne.

DESCRIPTION OF AN EMPIRICAL STUDY

Three different two-semester French courses (using three different text books) were taught at the University of Kentucky from 1966 to 1969, all of them implementing the audio-lingual theory of foreign language learning. Two of the three courses were non-programmed, while a third one was programmed. In addition, two courses, both using *Basic French*[1] were taught, embodying cognitive code-learning principles. They were programmed like the third audio-lingual course mentioned above. The dates and character of these courses are summarized in Table 2.

TABLE 2. *French courses taught at the University of Kentucky from 1966 to 1969*

Classification	1st semester	2nd semester
Audio-lingual course 1	fall 1966	spring 1967
Audio-lingual course 2 (programmed)	spring 1967	fall 1967
Audio-lingual course 3	fall 1968	spring 1969
Cognitive code-learning course 1	spring 1968	fall 1968
Cognitive code-learning course 2	fall 1968	spring 1969

All five courses were taught by Graduate Assistants for whom this was their first teaching experience. They taught three recitation periods a week, while the author gave the weekly lecture. The author was responsible for two of the three audio-lingual courses (1 and 2), and for the two courses which used the cognitive code-learning approach. He visited the recitation sections, held regular meetings with the Graduate Assistants and administered the tests and the final examinations.

[1] Mueller and Niedzielski (1968).

According to the character of each course, the weekly lecture was based on either audio-lingual principles or cognitive code-learning principles.

The student body in each of these courses was essentially similar. The aptitude of the students was measured by the Carroll–Sapon Modern Language Aptitude Test during their first semester of the two-semester course.[1] Mean percentiles on this test ranged from a high of 51 (fall 1966) to a low of 35 (fall 1968). This was due to a ruling requiring that all students with two or more years of high school French not be permitted to enrol in the first semester of the two-semester sequence. As this rule was not in force at the time of the first course, the mean aptitude at that time was higher than later. This factor, however, is not thought to have seriously altered the composition of the class in its second semester, since the more able students were now placed into the second semester course. The placement test consisted of the MLA Cooperative Tests in listening and reading, and required a score at the 50th percentile level for admission into the third semester.

TEST RESULTS

The MLA Cooperative Tests (Form LA) of listening, reading and writing were administered at the end of the various courses, and the results are set out in Table 3.

TABLE 3. *MLA Cooperative Test results for five courses*

	Listening		Reading		Writing	
	Mean scores	%ile	Mean scores	%ile	Mean scores	%ile
Audio-lingual courses						
1	17	37	24	32	50	50
2	21.2	45	24.2	32	46.4	50
3	18.7	42	28	43	—	(56.7)[a]
Cognitive code-learning courses						
1	27.2	71	29.3	50	62.6	73
2	24.5	69	28.8	50	64.5	73

Note

[a] This percentile is for half of the class only; due to unfortunate circumstances, the raw scores of the whole class and the mean percentile of one half of the class were not available to the author.

[1] Carroll and Sapon (1959)

The results obtained in the audio-lingual courses, whether the course was programmed or not, are essentially alike. They are below or near the average norms obtained nationally and published in the *Booklet of norms* for the MLA Cooperative Tests. The results obtained in the cognitive code-learning courses are significantly superior in the listening and writing measures at or beyond the ·01 level. In reading they are significantly superior to the first two audio-lingual courses, but less significantly to the third audio-lingual course. Compared with the national norms, the results obtained in the cognitive code-learning courses are significantly superior to the average (50th percentile) at the ·01 level in listening and writing, but similar in reading.

A comparison between the results obtained in the second audio-lingual course and the results obtained in the cognitive code-learning courses is of particular interest, since the content of the three was identical: all three courses used *Basic French*, taught according to audio-lingual principles in 1967 and according to cognitive code-learning principles in 1968 and 1969. The results in all three measures are significantly superior at the ·01 level for the two cognitive code-learning courses over the results obtained in the audio-lingual course.

The following changes were made when *Basic French* was taught according to cognitive code-learning principles:

1. In class

(*a*) The grammatical explanations in the lectures were based on the 'Basic Sentence Patterns' as the integrating feature. Much more time and effort was spent explaining the patterns than had been the case before. The charts used in class were also handed out in dittoed form with the needed explanations for further study at home.

(*b*) The class work in the recitations was devoted to those exercises which tended to make the student generate sentences rather than manipulate them, to contrast a sequence of patterns rather than to repeat a single pattern.

2. Homework

(*a*) The speaking–writing sequence, essential in audio-lingual theory, was gradually changed to a writing–speaking sequence. The students were told to write out a number of responses to each exercise as homework prior to coming to the language laboratory. This resulted in a drastic reduction in attendance at the laboratory, with over half reporting that they went one-third of the time or not at all.

(*b*) Confirmation of each response, which, in the audio-lingual course, had been available in print in the right hand column of each page, was now available to the student after he made his response. The confirmation was printed in invisible ink and became visible with a stroke of a specially treated pen, called 'access'. The essential change, however, does not seem to lie in the novelty of 'access', but rather in the change of the learning sequence.

(*c*) Writing received much greater emphasis than in the audio-lingual course. In the order in which it was used in the learning process, it contributed to cognitive code-learning.

The above changes are not to be interpreted as a complete abandonment of all audio-lingual principles in the course. On the contrary, the program for Part I (Phonology) was based on operant conditioning, and was used without modification in both the programmed audio-lingual course and the cognitive code-learning courses. Furthermore, in Part II of *Basic French* (Morphology), pattern drills were available as homework and recommended to the weaker students, while the better ones were urged to limit themselves to the exercises based on cognitive code-learning principles.

It is interesting to compare the retention rates of the third audio-lingual course and the second cognitive code-learning course, which ran concurrently. The data on the number of students who persevered in each course are set out in Table 4.

TABLE 4. *Comparison of course retention rates*

	Cognitive code-learning course 2	Audio-lingual course 3
Enrolled in first semester	144 students	57 students
Re-enrolled in second semester	93 students	27 students
Finished second semester	88 students (61.1%)	25 students (43.4%)

The third audio-lingual course lost over 56% of its enrolment, while the parallel cognitive code-learning course lost less than 39%. Whether the programming features may have had some influence in favor of the latter course is difficult to ascertain. However, the records show that in a typical audio-lingual course it is not unusual for 40% of the enrolment either to withdraw or fail the first semester, a phenomenon observed at several institutions.[1] The programmed audio-lingual course in its first semester had 15% withdrawals and 25% failures (i.e. a grade of D or E). It is, therefore, rather doubtful whether the number of course completions was any better in any of the other courses. Course completions are a measure of learning efficiency, and favor the cognitive code-learning principles. Students re-enrol in the subsequent course when they feel that they can be successful, but stay away otherwise. Thus, their failure to re-enrol indicates diffidence or dissatisfaction with the audio-lingual approach. Pimsleur has demonstrated that poor auditory ability is the prime reason for a student's withdrawing from a language course.[2] Inability to hear and process the stream of sounds arouses feelings of anxiety and makes the course unpopular.

CONCLUSION

The study described above compares the results obtained from three audio-lingual French courses, each taught over a two-semester sequence, one of the three using programmed learning, with those obtained from two programmed courses based to a large extent on cognitive code-learning theory. The results were measured by the MLA Cooperative Tests, Form LA. In all three audio-lingual courses the results were not significantly different; they were below or near the average results obtained nationally. The results obtained in the programmed courses based on cognitive code-learning were superior to both the results of the audio-lingual courses and the national norms, significant at the ·01 level, in the listening and writing measures; in the reading test they were similar to the national norms, but superior to two of the three audio-lingual courses. A significantly larger percentage of students completed the two-semester sequence which emphasized cognitive code-learning principles.

These results do not permit the conclusion that in all areas of language learning the cognitive code-learning theory is necessarily superior to audio-lingual principles. The courses emphasizing cognitive code-learning also relied heavily on audio-lingual concepts in some areas,

[1] Mueller (1968).
[2] Pimsleur, Sundland, and McIntyre (1966).

particularly on operant conditioning in teaching phonology. Furthermore, audio-lingual pattern drills were available and recommended particularly to the less able students.

On the basis of these results it is suggested that some students might require a certain amount of the sort of drill recommended by behavioral psychologists, or might require a combination of exercises based on both audio-lingual and cognitive code-learning principles. A student with poor language aptitude is unable to remember sounds, and has difficulty associating them with their symbols. The author's study of programmed instruction, mentioned above, has shown that this difficulty can be overcome through operant conditioning. Drills which emphasize memory of a sequence of sounds and de-emphasize meaning might be more efficient for the less apt students. When one considers the disparity of student ability, it becomes quite clear that individualized learning is necessary. It is not only conceivable, but rather likely that the materials used to teach one type of student effectively will be unsuited for a different type. If it can be shown that certain types of drills are more effective with some students than with others, sequences could be established which are tailored to the individual's aptitude and thus ensure the best learning conditions.

BIBLIOGRAPHY

Carroll, John B. 'The contributions of psychological theory and educational research to the teaching of foreign languages.' In Valdman, *Trends*, pp. 93–106.

Carroll, John B., and Sapon, Stanley M. *The modern language aptitude test.* New York: The Psychological Corporation, 1959.

Ferguson, Charles A. 'Applied linguistics.' In Mead, Robert G. (ed.), *Language teaching: broader contexts (Northeast Conference on the Teaching of Foreign Languages, 1966. Reports of the Working Committees)*, pp. 50–8.

Mueller, Theodore H. 'Programmed language instruction – help for the linguistically underprivileged.' *The Modern Language Journal*, **52** (1968), 79–84.

Mueller, Theodore H., and Niedzielski, Henri. *Basic French – a programmed course.* New York: Appleton-Century-Crofts, 1968.

Pimsleur, Paul, Sundland, Donald M., and McIntyre, Ruth D. *Under-achievement in foreign language learning.* New York: MLA, 1966.

Rivers, Wilga M. *The psychologist and the foreign-language teacher.* Chicago: University of Chicago Press, 1964.

Valdman, Albert (ed.). *Trends in language teaching.* New York: McGraw-Hill, 1966.

12 Linguistic and psychological factors in speech perception and their implications for teaching materials

WILGA M. RIVERS

Speech perception, it must be admitted, is a subject about which very little is known with any certainty. How is it possible, we may ask, for a person to extract a message from a continuous stream of sound which trained phoneticians find difficult to segment when the acoustic signal is recorded on a spectrogram. Yet, despite linguists and psychologists, understanding utterances is the common experience of every normal human being, and despite our ignorance of its nature we continue to train students who can understand not only their native language but foreign languages as well.

There are many questions about speech perception for which at present we can expect no definitive answers. Some maintain that the reception of a message is determined by the operation in reverse of the same processes as those involved in its emission. For this view there is as yet little experimental evidence and some that would seem to refute it.[1] Others consider that we perceive an oral message by covertly constructing a parallel message with which we compare it for fit – if this is so, speech perception must be considered a special case of speech production. Still others consider speech perception a distinctive process in which the decoding rules draw on different factors from the encoding rules of speech production, with semantic cues playing a predominant role. Most linguists have concentrated on the system of rules which must be internalized if speech production is to be a theoretical possibility and Chomsky at least sees no difference between the knowledge of the

[1] Schlesinger (1968), chapter 6: 'Syntactic and semantic decoding.'

language which must be posited for hearing and for speaking. The model of such a system of rules is a description of competence with no pretence at describing performance.[1] Psychologists, on the other hand, must concern themselves with the behavioral reality of the systems of rules elaborated by linguists, attractive as these may be as theoretical models, and they cannot accept without experimental evidence identity of process in performance for the two aspects of the communication act. As applied linguists we are caught in the middle and for our practical purposes we may be led sorely astray if we accept a theoretical model as a representation of psychological reality without looking for experimental validation.

Many writers have classified the comprehension of speech as decoding, and left it at that. This term is deceptively simple for a process which involves first perceiving that there is a systematic message rather than accidental noise in a continuous stream of sound, then apprehending and identifying within this stream bounded elements (segments) which the listener has never heard in exactly this form before, each segment having a distinctive structure and combining with other segments within a more extensive organized system. As the listener seeks to interpret the message he is hearing, this structuring within and among segments requires that he retain elements he has already apprehended until their relationships with succeeding elements have been established, and that he then engage in a continuous readjustment of his interpretation of each developing structure in view of what has preceded and in anticipation of succeeding segments. The listener is thus engaged in a continuous process of analysis and synthesis, in which factors of attention and memory are vitally involved. Comprehending a message is not merely attending to a stream of sound and establishing some construction at the whim of the listener: there is a highly complex structured system involved which has an existence apart from this

---

[1] Chomsky (1965, p. 9): 'To avoid what has been a continuing misunderstanding, it is perhaps worth while to reiterate that a generative grammar is not a model for a speaker or a hearer. It attempts to characterize in the most neutral possible terms the knowledge of the language that provides the basis for actual use of language by a speaker–hearer. When we speak of a grammar as generating a sentence with a certain structural description, we mean simply that the grammar assigns this structural description to the sentence. When we say that a sentence has a certain derivation with respect to a particular generative grammar, we say nothing about how the speaker or hearer might proceed, in some practical or efficient way, to construct such a derivation.'

particular listener and speaker and which is known to varying degrees of complexity by both. Nor is comprehension the passive reception of an already structured message. Since the speaker and the listener in a communicative act are different persons whose competence in the language is never identical, it is quite possible for the message perceived to be structured differently from that intended by the speaker. With a message in a language which is not the native language of one of the two participants the discrepancy in competence may be considerable and the probability that the message perceived will be identical to the message emitted will be correspondingly reduced. The structure apprehended by the listener in the stream of sound will also be influenced by situational context and by such personal factors as set, fatigue and emotion. As a result, the message one person finally receives will not correspond precisely to the message another person would have perceived in the same communication sequence. Listening comprehension is an area in which linguistic and psychological factors are inextricably interwoven and as a phenomenon it can never be explained purely from the point of view of the psychologist or of the linguist. Insofar as it is a performance phenomenon it can be investigated empirically as behaviour (behaviour involving two persons), but such investigation will be peripheral unless it takes into account what the linguist has to say about competence and the organization of the language system.

There is reason to believe that the act of perception is not a purely passive one. It is an act of construction rather than of reception.[1] In continually varying sounds we recognize a phonemic system: combinations of sounds with certain complexes of distinctive features which we have come to accept within a certain band of tolerance as sounds of the particular language to which we think we are listening. Should we anticipate that an utterance will be in a specific language, we will not perceive the same combinations of sounds as we would have perceived if we had been expecting another language, although the sound signal itself will not have changed. As we listen for a particular language we will not be disconcerted by variations in sound sequences which represent the same morphemes because we have internalized a system of morphophonemic rules which enable us to adjust our construction appropriately beneath the level of conscious attention and effort – we are,

[1] For a full discussion with supporting experiments, see Neisser (1967), chapter 7.

however, 'hearing' the variants even if these are not made distinctly because this is what learning this language has made us expect.

Beyond this, we perceive in a continuous sound signal units and groups of units which as yet no machine has been able to identify consistently except when utterances have been shaped to conform to certain restrictions which suit its programme. These segments are perceived by the listener as belonging to groupings which possess a meaning at a deeper level of analysis because of the categories to which we assign the whole, and often parts, of each segment and because of the interrelationships we perceive among these categories, categorization extending to larger and larger internally structured segments until the ultimate category of the discourse itself is reached. The groupings we perceive form a rhythmic pattern which helps us retain what has been apprehended in earlier groupings long enough to interrelate it with later groupings in such a way as to make the utterance meaningful. When we know a language well, these rhythmic groups seem to form a pattern of rise and fall of the voice in harmony with meaningful content which may itself be a construction of the mind, rather than an uncontestable acoustic fact, as certain recent experiments seem to indicate.[1] Lieberman hypothesizes that it is meaningful content which suggests to us an appropriate learned intonation pattern in some cases so that we perceive what we expected even when the speaker has deviated from what we had anticipated.

We can detect in the process of perceptual construction three stages which should be kept in mind in the designing of teaching materials. The first stage, sometimes called 'sensing', is a stage of rapid impressions, only roughly identified and differentiated and is relatively passive and receptive. At this stage we impose some rudimentary segmentation on what we hear. We are dependent on echoic memory which is very fleeting (it has been estimated to last for a few seconds), so actual items heard are not long retained unless they are interrelated in some meaningful way with other items. The rapid synthesis of impressions which we form is a construction resulting from our familiarity with the phonemic system, the morphophonemic rules and the broad syntactic categories. As a result, much of what we have actually experienced auditorily does not pass on to the second stage because in our first rapid selection we have rejected as 'noise' elements which did not fit in with our initial construction. These sensory items then pass from echoic memory and can have no further effect on our interpretation.

[1] Lieberman (1965).

The second stage is one of identification through segmentation and grouping. We segment and group at various levels as we apply the phonotactic, syntactic, and lexical collocational rules of the language to which we are attending. This identification is not the identification of an input identical with that of previous auditory experiences, since what we are identifying we may never have heard in exactly that form before. It consists of an identification of configurations of attributes which distinguish categories, and then of wider categories of which the already identified categories are the attributes. In this way associations are aroused within the centrally stored information system. This identification process is an active, detailed one which processes the signal it is receiving sequentially, interrelating the segments it has already identified and those it is identifying within the phrase structure of the utterance. At this stage memory is still auditory, but because of the initial grouping in a rhythmic form which is tentatively meaningful, insofar as the phrase structure has as yet been apprehended, the auditory segments (or 'chunks' in G. A. Miller's terminology) are more easily retained.[1] It is because of this greater power of retention that we can suspend judgment where there is ambiguity of structure, holding perceived segments in our mind, ready to make the necessary adjustments as the form of the phrase structure becomes clear.

There is considerable discussion as to whether this process is one of analysis–by–synthesis. It seems difficult to explain the conversion of auditory information, received from outside the nervous system, into cognitive meaning. According to the analysis-by-synthesis hypothesis, as we listen we construct a parallel message within our own cognitive system, according to the organized rules we have internalized, and compare it for match, or fit, with what we are perceiving aurally. This hypothesis seems to tally with our common experience of supplying words when others pause, or of believing we are following with comprehension another person's message when suddenly we are disconcerted by the next element and have to revise our projection of the form of the utterance. The hypothesis is in some ways an attractive one, but as yet a satisfactory model of the process which could operate in real time has not been developed. Further, analysis-by-synthesis cannot explain common substitution errors. If the input on which our matching is based is an acoustic signal, then it should be impossible to 'hear' words which have not been uttered, yet this is a common experience springing

[1] Miller (1956).

from our projection of the probable form of the utterance to which we are attending. It seems plausible, therefore, that we are engaged as we listen in some form of anticipatory projection, with adjustive correction should the utterance not conform with our expectations. This projection is based on our familiarity with the phrase structure, morphology and lexical collocations of the particular language to which we are listening, as well as the extra-linguistic factors of situation and gesture. The less familiar we are with these elements the more difficult we find it to comprehend and retain what we hear because of our inability to anticipate appropriately. The development of an adequate model of comprehension must, however, await more substantial knowledge of the actual processes involved from the psychological point of view.

Whatever may be the precise nature of the identification process, we would not remember what we had perceived were it not for the third stage, that of rehearsal and recoding of the material, which must take place before what we have perceived enters into long-term storage. (Although this is called here a 'third stage' it must be considered as taking place simultaneously with the ongoing interpretative process.) Rehearsal refers to the recirculating of material through our cognitive system as we relate it to what follows and at times readapt what we have already interpreted in what we have already heard. Without rehearsal the auditory material in the memory would fade very rapidly and we would not be able to follow the line of thought in an utterance or series of utterances. It seems, however, probable that we do not store the material exactly as we first perceived it; rather we recode it in a more easily retainable form. A number of experiments seem to support the hypothesis that long-term storage (after thirty seconds) is in deep structure form:[1] that is, that the material perceived is detransformed and the basic semantic information retained, perhaps with transformational markers which enable the listener to recapture the original form if necessary. This hypothesis is consistent with common experience: when asked about what we have heard, we tend to give the gist of it, usually in simple active affirmative declarative sentences (which are referred to in the literature as SAAD). Such sentences are closest to base strings to which obligatory transformations only have been applied. It is optional transformations (such processes as passivization, nominalization and self-embedding) which seem to be dispensed with for storage although the semantic markers of such transformations as affect meaning (e.g.

---

[1] Fodor and Garrett, in Lyons and Wales (1966), pp. 148–51.

question, negation) are retained in the base. A series of simple kernel-like utterances is more redundant than utterances with a number of trans-formations which combine information and this redundancy aids memory. Recoding for retention must be performed immediately and without conscious attention or the listener misses part of the next grouping while he is rehearsing the recoding of the preceding segments. It is through recoding that the listener clarifies interpretatively relation-ships between what is being attended to and what has already been assimilated, and this establishing of meaningful associations is essential to storage and later recall.

At this point it is interesting to consider Fillmore's proposal that grammatical subject and object are surface features.[1] Real meaning is in the deep structure: not only the semantic contribution of the lexicon, but also the semantic aspect of syntactic relations. It is of interest that in psychological experiments on recall, the logical subject as expressed in an agent *by*–phrase has proved to be a more effective prompt than a non-agent *by*–phrase,[2] which seems to indicate the psychological reality of Fillmore's Agentive and to give added support to the notion that information is stored in deep structure form.

The three stages in speech perception which have been described form in practice one complex operation. It is reasonable, however, to presume that the efficiency of the whole process will be increased if listening comprehension materials are so constructed that the student has specific practice in the various types of operations he must perform almost automatically in an integrated series if he is to comprehend speech at a normal speed.

It has sometimes been suggested that students should begin the study of a foreign language by being plunged into a 'bath' of foreign language speech, that for some time they should listen only until they begin to absorb the language through continual exposure. (This has also been termed the 'sunburn' approach.) In the light of our analysis of the processes of speech perception, this method has little to recommend it. If the segmentation we make in the initial stages is vital, and if ready comprehension is to some extent dependent on our ability to project an anticipated message, then all that the 'sunburn' procedure can do is to familiarise the student to some extent with the general sound aura of

[1] Fillmore, in Reibel and Schane (1969).
[2] Blumenthal (1965), as described by Wales and Marshall in Lyons and Wales (1966), pp. 70–1.

the language, not the significant sound patterns, and encourage an attempt at segmentation based on native-language habits. It is our competence in the foreign language which enables us to segment and group meaningfully. Where the student does not as yet possess some degree of competence, he may be able to perform some rudimentary semantic decoding where mime and visual images are introduced to supply clues to meaning, but it is then not clear to what degree the student is merely decoding the visual or kinesthetic signal system. With this prop removed he may remember some precise associations of specific phrases but he will have learned little upon which he can later build a system of decoding.

It is hardly a great step forward, however, to suggest that listening comprehension will grow as competence in the language is established. We can do better than that.

The first stage of speech perception is one of rapid, fleeting impressions, crudely segmented before the echo of the stimulus has disappeared from the memory. The initial selection is vital and normally related to syntactic groupings. (Where the structure is complicated the listener may resort momentarily to the less certain ground of purely semantic decoding, which in its simplest form is based on the order of semantic elements and their probable relationships.) We can help the student at this stage by ensuring the prolongation of the auditory image.

In the early stages students should be encouraged to repeat to themselves the segments they have apprehended, first as stretches of sound, then in an attempt at syntactic grouping. The very effort of repetition forces the student to segment the stream of sound in some fashion, the auditory image is longer retained, and the student has time to relate segments and to readjust his developing interpretation. Experiments at Harvard have shown that speech can be speeded up within segments and still be comprehensible so long as the pause between segments which is essential for cognitive processing, is slightly lengthened, so that the actual rate of presentation is not increased.[1] The student should be trained to use the pause for conscious processing, until early segmentation has become automatic. Early listening comprehension materials should, then, be kept within the limits of structural patterns being learned, so that rapid identification of syntactic groupings is possible Once the

[1] Harvard, C. C. S., *Sixth Annual Report*, p. 18, and *Seventh Annual Report*, pp. 30–1.

130

student has made an incorrect segmentation, he has lost the sound image and further adjustments must be made by conjecture and inference. Training in listening comprehension by parallel production is more than mere imitation: it forces concentration on segmentation as well as providing guided practice in the production of well-formed segments, thus integrating with listening comprehension an operation which is basic to creative speech production as well.

At the next stage, the student must identify more precisely and interrelate the segments he is holding in his short-term memory. Unless he is able to interrelate these meaningfully into larger groupings he will lose what he has so far retained. This is where the student will gain from systematic training from the beginning in the recognition of structural features. If he is ever to reach an advanced stage of listening comprehension where he can enjoy and later discuss all kinds of materials, he will need to be adept at rapid recognition of many indicators of structure. He must be able to categorize words and word groupings (in the practical sense of recognizing their function). He must be able to recognize rapidly sentence shape by identification of clues to question form, negation, coordination, subordination. He must recognize clues which indicate condition, purpose, temporal relationships. Such features are frequently signalled by initial words which should be apprehended immediately so that the mind can concentrate on less clearly marked syntactic relationships. He must be able to recognize rapidly signals such as prepositions, articles, and auxiliaries which help him discern constituents of phrase structure, and he must identify immediately in order to discard them prop words and hesitation words which add nothing to meaning but take up precious storage space (e.g. 'vous voyez', 'd'ailleurs', 'effectivement'; 'kind of', 'you know', 'I think'). Students should have frequent practice in repeating as units in meaningful contexts word groups of high frequency which contrast with those of their own language, and further practice in detecting these in listening materials. Exercises can be designed especially for practice in apprehending and matching orally certain types of structure (e.g. left-branching, right-branching, or nested constructions). Progressively developed these can be amusing exercises for laboratory practice. Once the student has been trained to listen purposefully and can identify readily the various clues to syntactic interrelationships which have been listed, his mind and memory will be free to concentrate on the lexical content of the message, using what he knows of reality to supply meaning when his knowledge of the foreign lexicon fails him.

Next there is recoding for retention. Here we may gain some ideas for teaching materials from the suggestion that information perceived aurally is detransformed for storage and is mostly recalled in simple active affirmative declarative sentences. We can aid the automatization of this process by giving students direct practice in such recoding. It is surface structure in the foreign language which is troublesome to the student because it is here that languages are differentiated and contrast. The student needs practice in detecting the main relationships (in Fillmore's terms the agentive, objective, instrumental, locative, among others); he needs training in abstracting these from the complications of the surface form and reducing the relationship extracted to a more basic form of expression: in other words he needs practice in giving the gist of what he hears in simple form. This he can then store, leaving his mind free to concentrate on incoming information. Exercises should be developed which force recognition of such deep structure relationships by using as prompt words for recall those which correspond to the agent, instrument or objective. It is the deep structure relationships which constitute language universals and in the recognition of these relationships the student is able to draw on his cognitive abilities beneath the level of surface structure complications. Students should also be given exercises in which they are presented first with the essence of what they are to hear in basic, kernel-like sentences and are then required to listen to the same substance in more complicated form with numerous transformations. Students who are not trained to decode and recode in the foreign language will inevitably develop the habit of automatically converting what they hear into a simplified form in the native language, thus wasting much valuable time and energy in translation and re-translation and never developing speed and ease in direct comprehension.

One of the perennial problems in modern language teaching has been the development of fluent direct reading. Students have been trained to read fluently recombinations of foreign-language speech they have learned, and even carefully graded readers kept within specified limits of known vocabulary and structure, but when they are finally allowed to read less controlled materials it becomes apparent that they have not developed a technique for extracting meaning directly from the foreign-language text. Many fall back into mere translation; others adopt a predominantly semantic strategy, seizing on lexical elements they recognize here and there and constructing some garbled version which shows they have not understood the basic structuring of the meaning. Research into the act of reading for meaning has shown that the processes involved parallel those of listening comprehension: first, there is recognition in a fast impressionistic way of segments which for comprehension must be identified as meaningful segments of phrase structure; there is the necessity to interrelate these according to basic relationships, holding one segment in the mind and suspending judgment until other segments are identified and combined with it in a meaningful way.

There is the same need for rapid recognition of categories, of sentence shapes, of markers, of constituents of phrase structure and for penetrating beneath surface complications to basic relationships. In view of this similarity of processes, the teaching of fluent reading could be considerably facilitated by combining it with a programme of training in listening comprehension. The effort at rapid segmentation (the identification of the essential relationships of the underlying phrase structure), the holding of chunks in the memory while awaiting confirmation of anticipations (that is, while waiting to see that the projected sentence is congruent with the actual sentence), the extracting of the gist (that is, the reduction to deep structure): all of these operations must be performed again in relation to the graphic medium. When the student is being trained in these specific operations for listening comprehension he should be made to realize their applicability to the other medium by being encouraged to read rapidly material based on the same content as what he has heard, and at other times to listen to oral presentations based on similar content to what he has read. The reading should not be done aloud, however, since hearing himself read and concentrating on how he is reading hinder the student in his rapid identification of the graphic symbol.[1]

Similar exercises to those outlined for listening comprehension should be developed for reading comprehension: reading the gist in simple active affirmative declarative sentences before reading a highly transformed version, practice in recounting in detransformed form what has been read, practice in detecting the deep structure relationships beneath the surface forms, rapid identification of cue words to structure and sentence shape. This is another whole area of concern and must be set aside for another paper. All good teaching, however, is teaching for

[1] Harvard C.C.S., *Seventh Annual Report*, p. 32.

transfer (or, as in this case, transposition), and teaching of listening comprehension should be no exception.

BIBLIOGRAPHY

Chomsky, Noam. *Aspects of the theory of syntax*. Cambridge, Mass.: M.I.T. Press, 1965.

Fillmore, C. J. 'Toward a modern theory of case.' In Reibel and Schane, 1969, pp. 361–75.

Fodor, J., and Garrett, M. 'Some reflections on competence and performance.' In Lyons and Wales, 1966, pp. 135–79.

Harvard Center for Cognitive Studies. *Sixth Annual Report 1965–66*.
Seventh Annual Report 1966–67.

Lieberman, P. 'On the acoustic basis of the perception of intonation by linguists.' *Word*, 21 (1965), 40–54.

Lyons, J., and Wales, R. J. (eds.). *Psycholinguistics papers: proceedings of the 1966 Edinburgh Conference*. Edinburgh: Edinburgh University Press, 1966.

Miller, G. A. 'The magical number seven, plus or minus two.' *Psychological Review*, 63 (1956), 81–97

Neisser, U. *Cognitive psychology*. New York: Appleton-Century-Crofts, 1967.

Reibel, David A., and Schane, Sanford A. *Modern studies in English – readings in transformational grammar*. Englewood Cliffs, N.J.: Prentice-Hall, 1969.

Schlesinger, I. M. *Sentence structure and the reading process*. The Hague: Mouton, 1968.

13   *Psycholinguistic universals in the reading process*[1]

KENNETH S. GOODMAN

Reading is a psycholinguistic process by which the reader, a language user, reconstructs, as best he can a message which has been encoded by a writer as a graphic display.

Through research on children reading English who are native speakers of some dialect of American English, I have evolved a basic theoretical view of the reading process. I hope it will be understood that some of what I will be saying is an extension of and projection of my theoretical view into dimensions that go beyond the research on which it is based. In this sense what I will say is hypothetical and I invite other scholars to test and challenge the hypotheses in terms of languages and orthographies other than English.

GENERATIVE AND RECEPTIVE ASPECTS OF LANGUAGE

It is ironic that although most researchers agree that receptive control of aspects of language precedes generative control more attention has been given to the process of language production than to the process by which language is understood. Many linguists have assumed that listening and reading are simply the mirror images of speaking and writing. They have assumed that since generative processes begin with meaning and result in a fully formed phonological or graphic display that receptive processes begin with the encoded display and reverse the process, step by step, to get back to meaning.

In this too simple view not enough consideration has been given to the variant nature of the productive and receptive tasks that are involved in language use. *In producing language*, the language user has thoughts which he wishes to express. In a transformational view, he creates a deep

---

[1] This paper has already appeared in *The Journal of Typographic Research*, **4** (1970), and is reprinted here by permission of the editor of that journal.

language structure which represents his meaning, applies a set of compulsory and optional transformational rules and generates a surface structure. If the language user is literate this surface structure may utilize a phonological signal and require the application of a set of phonological rules or it may utilize a graphic signal and require use of a set of orthographic rules.

The choice will be dictated, of course, by the language user's purpose. The receptive process does start with the phonological or graphic display as input, and it does end with meaning as output, but the efficient language user takes the most direct route and touches the fewest bases necessary to get to his goal. He accomplishes this by *sampling*, relying on the redundancy of language, and his knowledge of linguistic constraints. He *predicts* structures, *tests* them against the semantic context which he builds up from the situation and the ongoing discourse and then *confirms* or disconfirms as he processes further language.

Receptive language processes are cycles of *sampling, predicting, testing* and *confirming*. The language user relies on strategies which yield the most reliable prediction with the minimum use of the information available.

Neither listening nor reading is a precise process, and in fact even what the language user perceives is only partly what he sees or hears and partly what he expects to see or hear. This is necessarily so not only because of the prediction in which the language user engages but also because he has learned to organize his perceptions according to what is and is not significant in the language. The language user must not simply know what to pay attention to but what not to pay attention to.

The producer of language will be most successful if the signal he produces is complete and well-formed. With such a signal, the receiver of language is free to utilize his sampling strategies.

The necessary concern for oral language which had been neglected for so long caused many scholars to dismiss written language without adequate consideration as a secondary representation of oral language. But written language in a literate culture is not simply a way of preserving and recording oral language. It designates streets, places, and directions, it labels and classifies. It makes communication possible over time and space.

A key difference between oral and written language is that speech is most commonly encountered within the situations in which it is most relevant. Speakers may rely on the situational context to make referents explicit. Listeners may infer from the situational context and from the movements, actions, and gestures of speakers a great deal of semantic information to augment and constrain what they derive from the language.

Written language tends to be out of situational context. The writer must make referents and antecedents explicit, he must create contexts through the language to replace those which are not present. He must furthermore address himself to an unseen and frequently unknown audience. He gets no immediate linguistic or visual feedback to cue him as to whether his communicative efforts are successful.

Written language is perfectible in that the writer may edit it to be sure he has said exactly what he wished to say. It is not perishable in the sense that oral language is.

These differences should not obscure the basic similarities between the alternate language forms for literate language users, but they should make clear that reading and listening will employ variant psycholinguistic strategies to cope with the variant characteristics of the two forms. Reading employs a strategy of regression to reread, for example, whereas listening cannot employ a comparable strategy. The listener must ask the speaker to repeat and that is not always feasible.

One misconception which has caused considerable confusion in dealing with the reading process is the notion that meaning may only be derived from oral language. It is assumed by some that readers engage in a process of recoding graphic input as aural input and then decoding. While this may in fact take place in beginning stages of the acquisition of literacy among some learners, it is not necessary or characteristic of proficient reading. An analogy can be found in the early stages of learning a second language. The learner may be going through a process of continuous translation into his first language before he decodes. But eventually he must be able to derive meaning directly from the second language with no recourse to the first. Just so the proficient reader becomes as skillful at deriving meaning from written language as he is from the aural form with no need to translate one to the other.

It must be remembered that oral language is no less an arbitrary code than written language. Neither has any direct relationship to meaning and the real world other than that which its users assign it.

Alphabetic writing systems have a number of virtues among which is that there is a built-in correspondence to the units and sequences of the oral language form. But this is not an unmitigated blessing. A writing system which is directly related to ideas and concepts has the virtue that it can be used for communication by speakers of different languages.

The system of mathematical notation has that advantage. $6 + 9 = 15$ is a mathematical statement that will be immediately understood by speakers of a wide range of languages, whereas six and nine equal fifteen can only be understood if the reader knows English.

The Chinese writing system may indeed have its faults but it has the virtue of being understood by speakers of oral languages which are not mutually comprehensible. And of course the Chinese writing system, once it is mastered, does function quite well for its users. Alphabetic writing systems are not in fact necessary for literacy.

THE READING PROCESS

The readers of English I have studied utilize three cue systems simultaneously. The starting point is graphic in reading and we may call one cue system *graphophonic*. The reader responds to graphic sequences and may utilize the correspondences between the graphic and phonological systems of his English dialect. I should point out that these are not phoneme–grapheme correspondences but in fact operate on morphophonemic levels (that is, spelling patterns relate to sound sequences). In English as in other languages the spelling system is fixed and standardized. This means that correspondences will vary from dialect to dialect and that, over time, changing phonology will loosen the fit of even the tightest alphabetic system.

The second cue system the reader uses is syntactic. The reader, using pattern markers such as function words and inflectional suffixes as cues, recognizes and predicts structures. Since the underlying or deep structures of written and oral language are the same, the reader seeks to infer the deep structure as he reads so that he may arrive at meaning.

The third cue system is semantic. In order to derive meaning from language the language user must be able to provide semantic input. This is not simply a question of meaning for words but the much larger question of the reader having sufficient experience and conceptual background to feed into the reading process so that he can make sense out of what he is reading. All readers are illiterate in some senses, since no-one can read everything written in his native language.

These cue systems are used simultaneously and interdependently. What constitutes useful graphic information depends on how much syntactic and semantic information is available. Within high contextual constraints an initial consonant may be all that is needed to identify an element and make possible the prediction of an ensuing sequence or the confirmation of prior predictions.

Proficient readers make generally successful predictions but they are also able to recover when they produce miscues which change the meaning *in unacceptable ways*.

No readers read material they have not read before without errors. It must be understood that in the reading process accurate use of all cues available would not only be slow and inefficient but would actually lead the reader away from his primary goal which is comprehension. In fact in my research I have encountered many youngsters who are so busy matching letters to sounds and naming word shapes that they have no sense of the meaning of what they are reading. Reading requires not so much skills as strategies that make it possible to select the most productive cues.

These strategies will vary with the nature of the reading tasks. For example literature has different characteristics than discursive language. The writer will use unusual terms and phrases rather than the more trite but also more predictable ones which would be used to express the same meaning in everyday conversation. The reader needs strategies that adjust to the very different constraints in literary materials.

Because reading involves visual input, characteristics of the visual system do affect the reading process. The material must be scanned from left to right as English is printed and the eye must focus at specific points since it cannot provide input while it is in motion. At each fixation a very small circle of print is in clear sharp focus. Some have argued that only print in sharp focus can be used in reading. But there is a large area of print in the peripheral field at each point of fixation which is not seen clearly but is sufficiently seen to be usable in the sampling, predicting and confirming aspects of reading. The reader can in fact work with partial, blurred, even mutilated graphic input to a considerable degree.

That, too briefly, is what my research has told me about the process of reading English among native American speakers. I have no reason to believe that this process would vary except in minor degrees in the reading of any language. Whether the graphic sequence is from left to right, right to left, or top to bottom would be of little consequence to the basic reading process. The reader needs to scan appropriately but he will still sample and predict in much the same way.

With alphabetical orthographies the regularity of correspondence rules for letter–sound relationships is not nearly as important as many people have believed. Readers are able to use syntactic and semantic cues to such a considerable extent that they need only minimal graphic cues in many cases. They can tolerate a great deal of irregularity, ambiguity, and variability in orthographies without the reading process suffering. There is in fact a wide range in which an alphabetic orthography may exist and still be viable. Only minor adjustments in the reading process are required to deal with any unusual correspondence features.

An example in reading English is the variability of vowel representation. This is particularly confused since the unstressed vowel schwa, may be spelled by any vowel letter. Readers learn to rely more heavily on consonants, particularly initial ones for their minimum cues and to use vowel letters only when other information is inadequate.

I confess to know nothing about problems of reading non-alphabetic writing systems but I strongly believe that readers of languages which employ them will still be sampling using minimal graphic cues to predict grammatical structures.

Grammatical patterns and rules operate differently in each language but readers will need to use their grammatical competence in much the same way. Some special reading strategies may result from particular characteristics of the grammatical system. Inflections are relatively unimportant in English grammar but positions in patterns are quite important. In a highly inflected language the reader would find it profitable to make strong use of inflectional cues. In English such cues are not terribly useful.

Semantic aspects of the reading process cannot vary to any extent from one language to another since the key question is how much background the reader brings to the specific reading.

To sum up it would seem that the reading process will be much the same for all languages with minor variations to accommodate the specific characteristics of the orthography used and the grammatical structure of the language.

LEARNING TO READ ONE'S NATIVE LANGUAGE

In the personal history of each individual in a literate society he learns first to control the spoken language and several years later to control the written language. He masters speech with no organized instruction. Normally he learns to read and write in school. It is puzzling that far less success is achieved in learning to read than in learning to speak.

Obviously there is not time to explore this vexing problem. But several key points need to be made:

1 Children who learn oral language should be able to learn to read.
2 Children who know oral language should be able to use this knowledge in learning to comprehend written language.
3 Reading instruction should center on comprehension strategies.
4 The reading process cannot be fractionated into sub-skills to be taught or subdivided into code-breaking and comprehension without qualitatively changing it.
5 Reading instruction should use natural meaningful language within the conceptual grasp of the learners. (This implies of course that the content should always be relevant as well.)
6 Where it is at all feasible the child should achieve initial literacy within his own language (in fact within his own home dialect!).

READING A SECOND LANGUAGE

Here are some implications I see from my study of the reading process for learning to read a second language:

(a) Learning to read a second language should be easier for someone already literate in another language, regardless of how similar or dissimilar it is.
(b) Reading will be difficult as long as the student does not have some degree of control over the grammatical system.
(c) Strong semantic input will help the acquisition of the reading competence where syntactic control is weak. This suggests that the subject of reading materials should be of high interest and relate to the background of the learners.
(d) Reading materials in early language instruction should probably avoid special language uses such as literature and focus on mundane, situationally related language such as signs, directions, descriptions, transcribed conversations, etc. This would depend of course on the background of the learner. Scientists should do very well with materials dealing with their own interests.
(e) It will always be easier for a student to learn to read a language he already speaks. For young learners this clearly suggests a

sequence of early focus on oral language and later introduction of reading, even in situations where the second language will be the medium of later education. But the motivation and needs of older highly literate students may suggest that oral and written language receive equal attention even at early stages.

(f) As in learning to read a first language reading instruction should always involve natural, meaningful language and instruction should avoid the trivial and keep the focus on comprehension strategies.

14 Experimental investigation of receptive language

ANNIE MEAR

Most language specialists have analyzed, almost exclusively, productive language, where both ends of the communication channel are studied as emitters rather than as receivers. Only a few of them recognize that mastery of a particular language involves mastery of a receptive as well as a productive repertoire related to the vocal stimuli of the given language, and acknowledge the fact that the two repertoires should, therefore, be established through respectively adequate methods.

In order to investigate this receptive facet of language I studied the establishment of receptive French verbal repertoires, in children whose first language was English. The target to be reached was to have the children emit appropriate motor responses to specific sets of French vocal stimuli. Only those motor responses which were already under appropriate stimulus control in their native English were dealt with in the experiment.

METHOD

Subjects

The four subjects were first graders, two boys and two girls, who were between six and seven years of age. They were considered by their respective teachers to be 'average' in their class as far as their school performance was concerned. Living in Montreal where both English and French are spoken, these children had certainly been exposed to French on the street and through the mass media; yet French was not spoken in their homes and no attempt had been made to teach them either to speak or 'understand' French. Their only language for communication was English.

Procedure

The experiment consisted of individual instruction conducted according to the principles of operant conditioning. In the experimental setting the motor responses of each subject were brought under the appropriate stimulus control of English vocal stimuli by providing the subject with reinforcing events made contingent upon his emission of criterion performances. Each successful response was systematically followed by S's receiving a poker chip which he could later exchange for candy, snoopy stamps or books. At the beginning of the experiment delivery of these items by E was designated a reinforcing event for the subjects because they were highly desired by all four subjects. Jumping, walking, running, sitting down, standing up, and turning around also became behaviors highly desired by the subjects once they had been brought under the appropriate stimulus control of French vocal stimuli. Smiles, praise, applause delivered by E upon the emission of criterion perform- ances also contributed to the establishment of the target repertoires in the four subjects. Aversive controls were limited to E's emission of *non* upon S's emission of inappropriate responses. This technique allowed me to shape and bring to high strength: (1) imitation of the E's motor response models upon E's simultaneous emission of the appropriate French vocal utterance; (2) emission by the S of the appropriate motor responses upon E's emission of specific French vocal stimuli; (3) S's responding to a large number of French vocal stimuli.

1. The establishment of control over imitation

In order for each English-speaking subject to acquire a repertoire of observable motor responses related to French vocal stimuli, imitation of E's motor responses – produced simultaneously with a French vocal stimulus – had to occur reliably. Only then could significant advances be made. At the outset of the experiment each S was told that E was going to utter vocal stimuli in French while producing simultaneously the appropriate motor response corresponding to the given stimulus. S was to emit a motor response identical to that emitted by E. S was also instructed to perform as quickly as possible after hearing and seeing E's performance. In the first two sessions, S was prompted to imitate the motor responses corresponding to one word utterances such as *marche, cours, saute* which were modeled by E.

Reliable and immediate imitation was obtained by systematic reinforcement of imitative responses. E presented a motor response model simultaneously with a French vocal stimulus. Each time the child imitated the motor response, he was reinforced. During the process of establishing control over imitation all forms of extraneous behavior were extinguished; attending to E was reinforced by presenting the motor response to be imitated only when S was looking at E and was ready to imitate the motor response model produced by E. As the probability of immediate imitation was greater when S was looking at E this procedure, which increased the frequency of attending, increased the number of immediate imitations. When S was reliably and immediately imitating the first motor response produced by E simultaneously with the appropriate French vocal stimulus, a new motor response was introduced simultaneously with its corresponding French vocal stimulus, and the above procedure was repeated. The two motor responses were then alternately presented with their appropriate vocal control in French. When the child was reliably imitating these two motor responses, new motor responses were presented interspersed with the two original responses. Usually by the second or third motor response, a general imitative response class had been established, i.e. the child was then reliably and immediately imitating any new motor response. E, for example, started by modeling a sitting down response, which was then followed by a standing up response, which, in turn, was followed by a running response. After these three motor responses had been brought under imitative control, S would immediately imitate the kinesthetic models for walking, jumping, and turning around, successively presented by E. In this manner, control over each child's imitative behavior was systematically established.

2. *Bringing motor responses from imitation control to French vocal stimulus control*

Bringing a given motor response under the control of a given French vocal stimulus involved shaping S to emit the appropriate motor response when presented with the French vocal control. After imitative responses occurred with high probability and short latency following each kinesic prompt stimulus control was shifted from the kinesic prompt to the vocal prompt alone, thus bringing S's motor responses under the appropriate stimulus control of French vocal stimuli.

Once reinforcement for imitation had produced a high probability of successful imitation of the motor response, the French vocal control was presented simultaneously with an ancillary hand movement, and S was reinforced for emitting the appropriate motor response. For example, in order to bring the child to emit an appropriate response when the French vocal utterance *saute* was emitted, E first presented the appropriate response for S to imitate; at the next stage, E would just point upwards to provide S with a visual cue, until finally the child's jumping response was emitted upon the mere emission of the French vocal utterance *saute*. The same procedure was followed for every motor response to be brought under the control of every French vocal utterance. For example, to make the child turn around when the vocal utterance *tourne* was emitted, E would first provide a motor response model to be simultaneously imitated by the child; then E would make a circular hand movement, until finally the child could respond appropriately to the vocal utterance *tourne*. For an utterance like *donne-moi le cheval rouge*, E first opened her hand in front of the designated animal, then looked toward the given plastic figurine, until the subject would emit the appropriate response upon E's emission of the above-mentioned vocal control alone.

Throughout the experimentation whenever the child emitted an inappropriate response, a time-out was programmed, i.e. E would say *non* and repeat the given French vocal stimulus; then the child usually produced a criterion performance; but if the second response produced by the child was still inappropriate, E looked down and after two or three seconds of silence went on to emit another French vocal utterance. This, in fact, only happened in a few instances.

Thus, if the experimental contingencies are properly managed, the process of bringing motor responses from imitation control to French vocal stimulus control is relatively effortless.

3. *The expansion of the receptive repertoire related to French vocal stimuli*
After S had been trained to emit several appropriate observable motor responses upon E's emission of specific French vocal stimuli, any motor response already under the appropriate stimulus control of English vocal stimuli could be brought rapidly under the control of the corresponding French vocal stimuli. However, it should be noted that the child would sometimes not respond appropriately to a given French vocal stimulus at the beginning of the next daily session or subsequent to learning to emit an observable motor response to a new French vocal stimulus in the same session. A motor response was considered to be under the appropriate stimulus control of a specific French vocal

utterance only when the child could emit the given response after other responses had been established and following a passage of time. That target was reached by gradually changing the context in which a specific French vocal control was presented. After a child was consistently emitting appropriate motor responses upon E's presentation of particular French vocal utterances, S was presented with a French vocal stimulus for which he had previously been trained to emit an appropriate motor response. When S emitted the appropriate observable motor response to the previously 'learned' French vocal control he was reinforced and the new French vocal stimulus was presented again.

E decided to establish first motor responses corresponding to one-word utterances and to proceed from there to the establishment of responses corresponding to longer and longer utterances. In those instances where S had to be trained to such units as *mets le cheval rouge et le cheval blanc dans la boîte*, the procedure was the same as in establishing appropriate responses to one-word utterances such as *cours, marche, saute, assiedstoi, lève-toi*. The task that faced E in such a case was to break down the utterance into minimal units and for each of these units he must gradually establish in each S an appropriate response. For example, for the utterance *mets le cheval rouge et le cheval blanc dans la boîte*, he had to establish in S an appropriate response for *mets – le cheval rouge – et – le cheval blanc – dans la boîte*. Once this basic tenet of behavioral technology is clearly understood, there should be no limit as to the size of the receptive repertoire related to foreign language vocal stimuli which can be established in any normal subject.

RESULTS AND DISCUSSION

The data collected in the experiment demonstrate that a receptive repertoire related to vocal stimuli in a second language can be established in a short period of time through systematic teaching.

Total time of contact between the experimenter and the subjects

Table 1 given below represents contact time between E and each S in each particular session, as expressed in minutes. It also represents the total time of contact between E and each S in particular during the length of the experimentation.

ANNIE MEAR

TABLE 1. *Length of each session and total time of contact between E and S for each particular subject, expressed in minutes*

Session	David	Kellie	John	Rosaleen
I	10	10	10	8
II	18	16	10	8
III	19	20	20	9
IV	30	22	23	23
V	24	28	26	27
VI	29	26	24	22
VII	24	24	23	27
VIII	32	26	15	24
IX	28	30	22	21
X	24	21	21	—
XI	30	30	33	—
XII	28	29	26	—
XIII	29	32	—	—
Total time of contact	325	314	253	169

Extent of the receptive repertoires established in the four subjects

One of the relevant questions to be asked of the data is the following: to how many French vocal stimuli was each subject trained to respond, (a) in each session, and (b) over the duration of the experiment? Table 2 summarizes this information.

TABLE 2. *Number of French vocal stimuli presented by E in each session to each particular subject*

Session	David	Kellie	John	Rosaleen
I	3	3	3	3
II	3	3	3	3
III	6	7	6	6
IV	8	8	7	8
V	15	11	16	17
VI	4	8	9	7
VII	7	6	8	34
VIII	12	14	12	13
IX	17	20	10	14
X	10	9	8	—
XI	16	30	21	—
XII	10	22	12	—
XIII	11	11	—	—
Total number of stimuli	122	152	115	105

Qualitative analysis of the receptive repertoires established in the four subjects

The four subjects were conditioned to respond appropriately to various types of French 'mands' which can be classified in eight major categories:[1]

1. *Mands for a total physical response*, on the part of the subject, such as *assieds-toi, lève-toi, cours, marche, saute, tourne*, to which the four Ss were trained to respond appropriately. See Table 3.

2. *Mands for 'pointing'*. All the mands in this category started with the French vocal utterance *montre-moi* and provided discriminative stimuli for S to point differentially to his nose, his mouth, his eyes. See Table 4.

3. *Mands for 'handing'*. All the mands in this category started with the French vocal utterance *donne-moi*. See Tables 5 and 6.

4. *Mands for 'placing' objects*. All the mands in this category were constructed on the pattern: *mets X dans Y*, or *mets X sur Y*. See Tables 7 and 8.

5. *Mands for 'putting X on' and 'taking X off'*. Kellie, for example, was conditioned to put on and take off headbands of various colors, responding to such vocal stimuli as: *mets le bandeau blanc* and *enlève le bandeau blanc*. See Table 9.

6. *Mands for 'opening' and 'closing'*. These mands were of the type *ouvre X* and *ferme X*. See Table 10.

7. *Mands for bringing X and taking X back*. To this class belong all the mands of the type: *apporte-moi X* and *remets X*. See Table 11.

8. *Mands for 'manipulating'*. In this class are found all the mands which required the S to manipulate things, as for example, cutting paper with scissors, folding paper, putting a piece of paper in an envelope, taking a napkin, throwing it away, emptying a glass of water, or a flask. A complete listing of the mands belonging to this class is provided in Table 12.

[1] The *mand*, according to Skinner (1957, p. 35), 'may be defined as a verbal operant in which the response is reinforced by a characteristic consequence and is therefore under the functional control of relevant conditions of deprivation or aversive stimulation.'

ANNIE MEAR

The results suggest that it might be very effective to teach a foreign language by establishing in the language learner *first* a receptive repertoire related to the foreign language the student wants to learn. The crucial point to be emphasized is the necessity of interim objectives in order to reach the final objective, i.e. mastery of a specific foreign language. The solution offered by this experiment is to deal with motor responses already in the student's repertoire under the control of vocal stimuli in his first language and to bring them progressively under the control of vocal stimuli in the second language. Only after the receptive repertoire has been established should the expressive repertoire be taken into consideration. This is, of course, only one alternative to the issue of language teaching. From the results of the experiment, however, it seems that the acquisition of a receptive repertoire prior to the introduction of the productive component of the language would constitute a most powerful advantage for the acquisition of adequate expressive behaviors.

BIBLIOGRAPHY

Skinner, B. F. *Verbal behavior*. New York: Appleton-Century-Crofts, 1957.

TABLE 3. *Mands for a 'total physical response'*

David	Kellie	John	Rosaleen
Assieds-toi	Assieds-toi	Assieds-toi	Assieds-toi
Lève-toi	Lève-toi	Lève-toi	Lève-toi
Cours	Cours	Cours	
Marche	Marche	Marche	Marche
Saute	Saute	Saute	Saute
Tourne	Tourne	Tourne	Tourne
Monte sur la chaise		Monte sur la chaise	Lave-toi les mains
Descends		Descends	Essuie-toi les mains
Assieds-toi par terre		Assieds-toi sur la chaise	
Assieds-toi sur la chaise		Va à la porte	
Lève le bras droit		Reviens	
Lève le bras gauche		Touche ton pied droit avec ta main droite	
Lève les deux bras		Touche ton pied gauche avec ta main gauche	
		Touche ton pied droit avec ta main gauche	
		Touche ton pied gauche avec ta main droite	

TABLE 4. *Mands for 'pointing'*

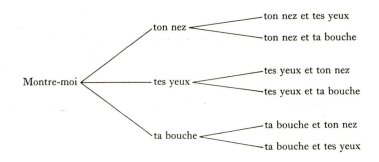

The mands shown in this table were presented to all four subjects.

TABLE 5. *Mands for 'handing' (color-related stimuli)*

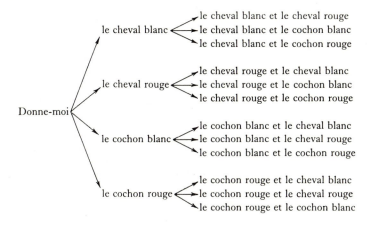

These stimuli were presented to all four subjects.

TABLE 6. *Mands for 'handing' (number and color-related stimuli)*

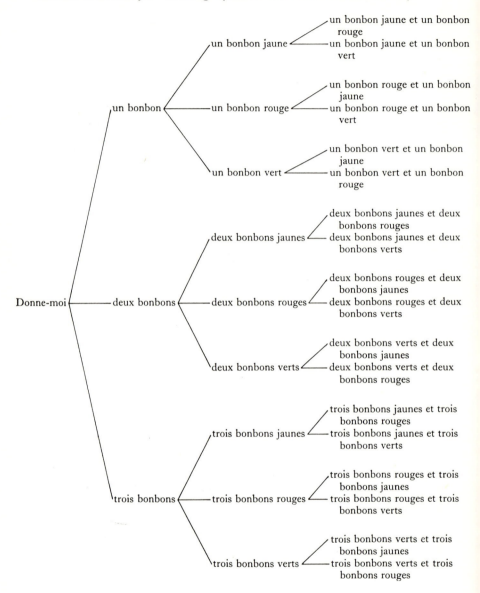

TABLE 7. *Mands for 'placing' objects*

Mets
- le cheval
  - *dans* la boîte – le cheval et le cochon dans la boîte
  - *sur* la boîte – le cheval et le cochon sur la boîte
- le cochon
  - *dans* la boîte – le cochon et le cheval dans la boîte
  - *sur* la boîte – le cochon et le cheval sur la boîte

These mands for 'placing' objects were presented to all four subjects. They became gradually more and more complex until they finally yielded the combinations presented in Table 8.

TABLE 8. *Mands for 'placing' objects*

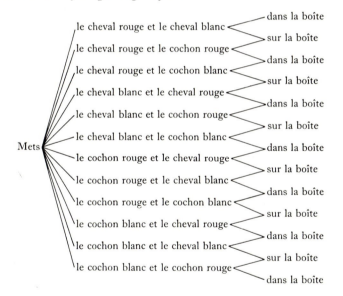

Mets
- le cheval rouge et le cheval blanc — dans la boîte / sur la boîte
- le cheval rouge et le cochon rouge — dans la boîte
- le cheval rouge et le cochon blanc — sur la boîte
- le cheval blanc et le cheval rouge — dans la boîte
- le cheval blanc et le cochon rouge — sur la boîte
- le cheval blanc et le cochon blanc — dans la boîte
- le cochon rouge et le cheval rouge — sur la boîte
- le cochon rouge et le cheval blanc — dans la boîte
- le cochon rouge et le cochon blanc — sur la boîte
- le cochon blanc et le cheval rouge — dans la boîte
- le cochon blanc et le cheval blanc — sur la boîte
- le cochon blanc et le cochon rouge — dans la boîte

This table presents a schematic view of the various combinations of stimuli to which the four subjects were conditioned to respond.

TABLE 9. *Mands for 'putting X on' and 'taking X off'*

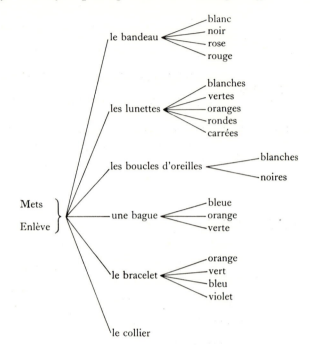

TABLE 10. *Mands for 'opening' and 'closing'*

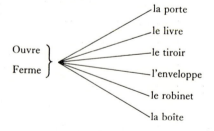

TABLE 11. *Mands for 'taking X' and 'bringing X back' to which John and David were conditioned to respond appropriately*

JOHN	DAVID
Apporte-moi un livre / Remets un livre	Apporte les bonbons
	Remets une cigarette
Apporte-moi deux livres / Remets deux livres	Remets deux cigarettes
	Remets trois cigarettes
Apporte-moi trois livres / Remets trois livres	
Apporte-moi un livre vert / Remets un livre vert	
Apporte-moi un livre rouge / Remets un livre rouge	

TABLE 12. *Mands for 'manipulating' to which David and Rosaleen were conditioned to respond appropriately*

David	Rosaleen
Coupe le papier avec les ciseaux	Prends une serviette
Plie le papier	Lance la serviette
Mets le papier dans l'enveloppe	Vide le verre
Ferme l'enveloppe	Vide le flaçon
Colle un timbre sur l'enveloppe	

15 Some actual and potential uses of rate-controlled speech in second language learning

HERBERT L. FRIEDMAN AND RAYMOND L. JOHNSON

I would like first to make it clear that this paper has not been written by a linguist, nor by an educator, so any complaints you may have about my treatment of language – or of learning – are probably valid. I will try rather to talk about listening behavior – to native as well as to foreign speech, and about a technique for altering recorded speech which has been used with some success in research, education, and information systems. It is my intention to inform you of this and to suggest some possible uses of this technique and of our research findings in the hope that some will indeed prove useful to second language learning, and that many others will be conceived of by you.

First, the technique. Rate-Controlled Speech, for all practical purposes, received its first impetus from the findings of Miller and Licklider (1950) that single, interrupted words remained intelligible in spite of the fact that as much as one half of each word was absent. This suggested to Garvey (1953*a* and *b*) that advantage might be taken not only of the redundancy in speech, but of the time no longer needed to present the interrupted segments. (If recorded speech is simply speeded mechanically, as you know, you get speech which is shifted upward in frequency – commonly called the 'Donald Duck effect' – and quickly becomes unintelligible.) He then proceeded by hand to remove minute segments of tape from a recording and paste the remainder together. I understand he has since developed something of an aversion to the subject. The playback of that tape was time-compressed speech without pitch distortion, and proved to be highly intelligible in spite of its shortened duration. At a rate of presentation two and one-half times the normal rate, the words remained about 80% intelligible. From his error analysis he concluded that his 'chopping' technique had damaged only 20 of the 442 speech sounds on the tape. Fairbanks, Everitt, and Jaeger (1954) then developed an electro-mechanical device for doing what Garvey had done by hand, and about the same time, in Germany, Anton Springer invented a similar device.

While a great deal of attention has since been given to better methods of time compression – preferably a method which deletes nothing – the only readily available devices still use the deletion technique for speeding, and the doubling of discard segments for expansion (or slowing). By this technique, what is discarded is random with respect to the content of the tape, although the size of the discard may be manipulated. A promising variation of computer-produced tapes (which are capable of somewhat more selective discarding if only someone will tell them what to discard) presents the discarded segment to one ear while the other receives the sample, i.e. dichotically, thereby restoring to the ear all the information when the rate is doubled, and an additional one-third when the rate is trebled (Scott, 1965). However, given the current state of 'field' machines about double rate is readily achieved and for native speech remains highly intelligible without training.

Fairbanks, with Guttman and Miron (1957) then studied compressed connected discourse, rather than single words, and found that while at 60% compression (about 353 words per minute for the technical information passage they used) the performance of listeners was about 50% of maximum; at 50%, or 282 wpm, response was almost 90% of maximum. Emerson Foulke (Bixler, Foulke, Amster and Nolan, 1961) then began a series of studies exploring the intelligibility and comprehension of time-compressed speech for the blind – for whom the savings in time in oral presentation is of enormous value since the faster visual channel is closed. He too found comprehension intact to about double speed. In 1963 (Orr, Friedman, and Williams, 1965) we, at the American Institutes for Research, in Washington, began our research into the possibility of training listeners to process speech at rates beyond those which they can accomplish at initial exposure. In the first studies, from a baseline speed of 175 wpm using college level history textbook material, we presented test passages at rates of 325, 375, 425, and 475 wpm at the end of each week with several hours' practice during the week listening to compressed light novels. At 325 and 375 wpm, experimentals did 85–90% as well as they had at 175 wpm, while controls (who had no

158

practice) managed 74–9% as well as normal. At 425 wpm, however, nearly two and one-half times the original speed, the decrement in performance was only 22–3% while control performance dropped below 50%. Similar studies performed during the next several years (Orr and Friedman, 1967, 1968; Orr, Friedman, and Graae, 1969) confirmed the trainability of compressed speech comprehension and also demonstrated that retention of content was as good for compressed tapes as it is for normal rates.

Two things clearly emerged from those early studies: (1) time-compressed speech was likely to prove a very valuable device for presenting information orally and could be used in a number of other ways, which I shall describe later; and (2) although comprehension for compressed discourse was feasible, and we could improve it, we did not know what the listener in fact did, to accommodate to faster speech, nor why some listeners were better at it than others. These questions remained in spite of our examination of a large number of stimulus and situational variables, including duration of exposure, the use of breaks in listening, key word lists and summaries prior to exposure, massed practice, the sex of the listener, and so on. We then asked (a little late, you may think) what the listener might do when speech time is compressed, and arrived at the following thinking.

Listening has many kinds of research and experience. Some of the ways in which it is selective have been explored in the dichotic listening experiments of Broadbent, Anne Treisman, and others. Anyone listening to a language in which he is not proficient knows that some portions of speech, for a variety of possible reasons, will not be adequately processed by him – the most common complaint is that the speech is too fast. But what do we mean by adequately processed? The activities which coincide with the stream of speech can be manifold. Features of the stimulus must be identified. They include physico-acoustic, phonemic, syntactic, and paralinguistic ones. The work that must be done on these may be variously described as identification, discrimination, matching, long and short-term storage, reiterating, paraphrasing, translating, comprehending, associating to, anticipating, and so on. Some of these activities are concurrent with the stream of speech. When that stream, containing the same linguistic content, is shortened in time three things can happen: (*a*) the listener can do all that he normally does, only faster; (*b*) he can eliminate or partially complete some of these activities; and/or (*c*) he can perform work on only selected aspects of the stimulus. The means to explore these questions were at hand in compressed speech, so we began to study, in a more molecular way than we had in the past, the behavior of listeners when speech processing time is reduced but intelligibility remains high. We began these studies in 1967 in native speech and also with students of a second language. They were a particularly intriguing group of listeners to consider since the work they must do on foreign speech is greater, and more time-consuming than for native speech. The second language project was conducted partly in Washington, and partly at the Defense Language Institute at Monterey, California, with students of Russian and Vietnamese, Hanoi dialect. The basic studies were performed in Washington with Russian students. In the paper which follows this some of the more successful ones will be described in detail. I will briefly mention one failure.

I have so far mentioned two major uses of rate-controlled speech – as a means of presenting information faster, and as a means of uncovering some of the basic characteristics of listening behavior by manipulating the temporal aspects of speech. A third possibility is to use it as a means of training listening. At Monterey we attempted to improve the ease of comprehension at normal speed by exposing students to gradually increasing rates of compressed speech – from just below normal to 1·6 times normal rate. An hour a day was presented, four days a week, for eight weeks, to Russian and Vietnamese students at three levels of proficiency. We found no major significant differences in performance between these students and a matched control group who heard the same material at normal rates. My feeling now is that the exposure was too limited, and the measures of performance too broad to get at possible listening changes. Subjectively, however, a majority of students and instructors felt that the compression exposure has been of some value.

I would now like, briefly, to mention six major categories of use, to which rate-controlled speech may be applied. I have discussed some which have been explored, but there are a number of others which I think merit some attention:

I. *As an information medium*
   (*a*) compressed speech may be used for processing or scanning to the advantage of
   (1) students
   (2) professionals – as is the case with the state medical association providing compressed lectures for their members

(3) for poor readers who may find listening a more satisfactory channel

(4) possibly for some people in listening to a second language for the same reason

(5) librarians and others who scan materials.

(b) At a slower rate for

(1) listening for comprehension in a foreign language

(2) those studying speech sounds in certain ways

(3) or – as a specific – it makes you sleepy.

II. *As a training device*

(a) Compressed

(1) I think the question of the usefulness of second language exposure to time-compressed speech remains open.

(2) It may provide a training technique for those who need to process language quickly, as for example interpreters, shorthand typists, radio operators, air traffic controllers, etc.

(3) One may also speculate that it could be of value in improving the cognitive processing of language and/or reading skill when used as a pacer, particularly if it is presented with judicious temporal spacing.

(b) Expanded

(1) It may be useful when slowed as a means of identifying speech defects by therapists or speakers themselves.

III. *Aptitude measurement*

(a) Compressed

(1) The nature of the skills which are needed for comprehension of time-compressed speech, which we have described elsewhere (Friedman and Johnson, 1968) are interesting ones. The ability to do this may serve as a predictor for some of the jobs I mentioned earlier, such as interpreter and air traffic controller.

(2) It might also serve to measure the proficiency of second language students or professionals. At what point, for example, does the highly proficient student have difficulty relative to the true bilingual?

IV. *Diagnostic device*

    (*a*) Compressed

        (1) The forced selectivity which compressed speech imposes on a listener may serve as an index of psychological or cognitive disorder if the content is so geared.

        (2) It may perhaps serve as a means for pinpointing listening and/or speaking deficiencies experienced by the second language student.

V. *Oral material difficulty index*

    (*a*) Compressed

        (1) When the listener is held constant, compressed versions of material which is equally difficult at normal speed may prove differentially difficult at high rates. Can that serve as a means of understanding language characteristics better?

VI. *As a basic research tool*

    (*a*) Compressed

        (1) Perhaps most interesting of all are the possibilities which are just beginning to be explored in the manipulation of this major temporal characteristic of speech in conjunction with linguistic and behavioral considerations. It may serve as a tool to identify priorities in the selectivity of perception by examining the nature and timing of responses to temporally adjusted speech.

BIBLIOGRAPHY

Bixler, R. H., Foulke, E., Amster, C. H., and Nolan, C. Y. *Comprehension of rapid speech by the blind.* Louisville, Ky.: University of Louisville Press, 1961.

Fairbanks, G., Everitt, W. L., and Jaeger, R. P. 'Method for time or frequency compression-expansion of speech.' *Transactions of Institute of Radio Engineers – Professional Groups* (1954), AU-2, 7–11.

Fairbanks, G., Guttman, N., and Miron, M. S. 'Auditory comprehension of repeated high-speed messages.' *Journal of Speech and Hearing Disorders,* **22** (1957), 20–2.

Friedman, H. L., and Johnson, R. L. 'Compressed speech: correlates of listening ability.' *The Journal of Communication,* **18** (1968), 207–18.

Garvey, W. D. 'The intelligibility of abbreviated speech patterns.' *Quarterly Journal of Speech,* **39** (1953), 296–306. (*a*).

'The intelligibility of speeded speech.' *Journal of Experimental Psychology*, **45** (1953), 102–8. (*b*).

Miller, G. A., and Licklider, J. C. R. 'The intelligibility of interrupted speech.' *Journal of the Acoustical Society of America*, **22** (1950), 167–73.

Orr, D. B., and Friedman, H. L. 'The effect of listening aids on the comprehension of time-compressed speech.' *The Journal of Communication*, **17** (1967), 223–7.

'Effect of massed practice on the comprehension of time-compressed speech.' *Journal of Educational Psychology*, **59** (1968), 6–11.

Orr, D. B., Friedman, H. L., and Graae, C. N. 'Self-pacing behavior in the use of time-compressed speech.' *Journal of Educational Psychology*, **60** (1969), 28–31.

Orr, D. B., Friedman, H. L., and Williams, J. C. C. 'Trainability of listening comprehension of speeded discourse.' *Journal of Educational Psychology*, **56** (1965), 148–56.

Scott, R. J. 'Temporal effects in speech analysis and synthesis.' Diss., University of Michigan, 1965.

16 *Some temporal factors in the listening behavior of second language students*

RAYMOND L. JOHNSON AND HERBERT
L. FRIEDMAN

One of the dominant topics in psychological studies of language in recent years has been the role of syntactic structure in the way we understand and remember sentences.[1] Syntactic structure does appear to affect perception and memory, although the experimental results are often conflicting or inconclusive. However, there is another approach to structuring – an approach more psychological than linguistic – which enables us to manipulate the speech event in a manner which considerably influences the accuracy with which listeners perceive and remember both individual sentences and connected discourse. This is structure in its temporal aspect: a grouping of the contiguous words in a sentence. The grouping is achieved by the selective insertion of temporal spaces or pauses at various locations within a sentence, locations which may or may not coincide with major syntactic junctures. We have recently completed a series of experiments in which we investigated the effects of temporal spacing when language is heard at accelerated rates, produced by the technique of speech compression. In the research we will describe today, we examine some of the effects of spacing and compression when the listeners are students of a second language, listening to speech samples of the language they are trying to learn.

[1] The research reported in this paper was performed under contract with the Advanced Research Projects Agency, Department of Defense. The authors acknowledge the assistance of Professor C.I.J.M. Stuart, University of Alberta.

METHOD

Materials

A set of sixty Russian sentences was constructed in such a way that the words making up the kernel or center of the sentence were contiguous and occurred either in the first or last half of the sentence. Correspondingly, the adjunct portion of the sentence (often a prepositional phrase) took up the remaining half. So, for thirty of the sentences the kernel preceded the adjunct and for thirty sentences, the adjunct preceded the kernel. The division of sentences into kernel and adjunct components was loosely based upon Harris' distinction (Harris, 1968), and had the advantage of yielding a more or less structural separation of the essential part of each sentence – its proposition or 'core meaning' – from the less essential qualifications and modifications.

The sentences were prepared using three versions of temporal spacing:

1. a *structurally segmented* version, where a space of about one second duration was inserted between kernel and adjunct.

2. a *non-structurally segmented* version, where a space was inserted between two words near the midpoint of the sentence, as determined by counting syllables. But the division did not coincide with the separation of kernel and adjunct, nor did the space mark any major phrase boundary.

3. a *non-segmented* version, where the sentence was uttered without interruption during a single breath group.

Sentences were presented to the listeners at one of two rates: a normal speaking rate of approximately 150 wpm, and a compressed rate. Naturally, the temporally spaced sentences were longer in overall duration than non-spaced sentences because of the added pauses. In an attempt to minimize the benefits of additional listening time which spacing provided, half of the sentences were compressed to a speed 30% faster than normal. This degree of compression so adjusted the playback times that – on the average – spaced sentences, when compressed, were equal in overall duration to non-spaced sentences presented at normal rate.

Subjects and procedures

Our subjects were thirteen college students who were enrolled in intermediate level Russian courses. These courses were taught using the customary audiolingual methods. The experiment itself was conducted in a language laboratory with students occupying individual booths. Their task was simply to listen to each sentence and immediately afterwards repeat it aloud as accurately as possible. In constructing the sentences, we carefully limited the vocabulary to those words which the students had already learned in their course work.

The design of the experiment required that half of the sentences be presented at normal rate, and half at the compressed rate. For each rate of presentation, one-third of the sentences were structurally spaced, one-third were non-structurally spaced, and a third were not spaced at all. For each of the three types of temporal spacing, half of the sentences were constructed in the kernel first-adjunct second pattern, and half were adjunct–kernel in composition. Thus, the experiment involved three variables, with five sentences representing each cell of the design. All subjects were exposed to all sentences, hearing those at normal rate before hearing the ones compressed. Within each rate of presentation the sentences were randomly scheduled with regard to the other two variables.

RESULTS AND DISCUSSION

For the initial data analysis, we were not concerned with the type of recall errors the subjects made. Rather we were interested simply in how many sentences were recalled with complete accuracy. Several analyses of variance yielded the following results:

First of all, we found that sentences with adjuncts at the beginning were recalled with significantly greater accuracy than were sentences beginning with a kernel ($F = 4.23$, 1 and 74 d.f., $p < 0.05$). This outcome agrees with two earlier findings: that kernels tend to be better remembered than adjuncts (indicating the selective nature of forgetting), and that the beginning of a sentence is better remembered than its end. This position effect perhaps provides some evidence to support the audio-lingual teaching technique known as the reverse build-up, where students memorize sentences backwards, from right to left. Our finding that a sentence was easier to recall if the adjunct occurred first can be explained by the fact that the part of the sentence most likely to be forgotten – the adjunct – was placed advantageously with regard to the position effect.

A second finding was that compression did not interfere with accurate recall. This result was surprising since we expected, on the basis of past experience, that an accelerated rate of presentation would impair performance. The absence of any effect can be partly attributed to the relatively slight degree of compression, but more substantially to the influence of temporal spacing.

The effect of temporal spacing was highly significant, both statistically and from the standpoint of psycholinguistics. The structural segmentation of sentences, inserting temporal spaces between the kernel and the adjunct, resulted in far more accurate recall than did either non-structural spacing or no spacing at all ($F = 7.08$, 2 and 72 d.f., $P < 0.01$). Non-structural segmentation was most productive of errors, probably because of some sort of interference, but the difference between the no-spacing condition and non-structural spacing was not large enough to be statistically significant.

Some insight into the reasons for the effect of temporal spacing was gained once we examined the nature of the recall errors which occurred when sentences were either structurally spaced or presented without spacing. When subjects tried to recall the unsegmented sentences they often had difficulty in getting to the end. The first few words would be recalled reasonably well, but then memory would fail and they would abruptly stop. In contrast, students trying to recall a structurally spaced sentence usually did manage to get to the end, in the sense that it was well-formed and complete grammatically and could be recognized as a sentence from its intonation pattern. The errors which occurred were meaning-preserving and usually involved omission or substitution. This difference in the likelihood of a subject's 'finishing' a sentence, however incorrectly, was statistically associated with the two conditions of spacing to a significant degree ($t = 3.17$, $P < 0.01$) and suggests that a structurally segmented sentence was perceived and remembered as a coherent linguistic entity while the non-spaced sentence tended to be heard merely as a string of weakly related words.

Such an interpretation is consistent with our previous findings concerning the effect of temporal spacing on perceiving and remembering sentences in one's native language (Johnson and Friedman, 1970). In a study using English sentences we found that those which had been structurally spaced were easier to remember than either non-structurally spaced sentences or sentences not spaced at all. This was especially true when the sentences were highly compressed to nearly three times normal rate.

We have also found that in the recall of sentences, adjectives are more likely to be forgotten than nouns. This differential memory for grammatical classes has been noted earlier by other investigators (Martin, Roberts, and Collins, 1968; Matthews, 1968), but we observed that the likelihood of an adjective being omitted is increased by any factor which makes the sentence difficult to remember, for example, length. As memory becomes burdened, forgetting becomes selective and adjectives tend to be omitted, perhaps because they are relatively less essential than nouns to the 'core meaning' of a sentence.

The effect of temporal spacing at structural junctures within the sentence is to reduce the rate at which adjectives are omitted. But spacing does not affect nouns, which are less likely to be forgotten anyway. We may infer, then, that structural spacing strengthens the bond in memory between a noun and its modifying adjective...that structural spacing reinforces the listener's ability to perceive and remember the relational properties of language.

BIBLIOGRAPHY

Harris, Zellig. *Mathematical structures of language*. New York: Interscience Publishers, 1968.

Johnson, R. L., and Friedman, H. L. 'Effects of temporal spacing on listening comprehension: a source of individual differences.' In Foulke, Emerson (ed.). *Proceedings of the Second Louisville Conference on Rate and/or Frequency Controlled Speech*. Louisville, Ky.: University of Louisville Press, 1970.

Martin, E., Roberts, K. H., and Collins, A. M. 'Short-term memory for sentences.' *Journal of Verbal Learning and Verbal Behavior*, **7** (1968), 560–6.

Matthews, W. A. 'Transformational complexity and short term recall.' *Language and Speech*, **2** (1968), 120–8.

17 Language communication and second language learning[1]

JOHN W. OLLER Jr

This paper is intended as a diagnosis of certain problems which have encouraged language teachers, especially in America, to parse language into 50,000 structural items (to use Dr Belasco's figure) while failing in many respects to see the sense and importance of realistic communicative use of the language in the classroom. Also it is partly a prognostication of future activities in second language learning theory and methodology which, incidentally, are already apparent in many of the discussions at this conference.

How we say something is intimately related to what it is that we wish to say. If this were not so, you and I could not understand each other. But we do. If we attempt to separate the 'how' of saying from the 'something' that is said, we run into difficulty. We cannot reasonably ask *how* something is said unless we presuppose *that* something is said. In other words, if we ask how something is said without already knowing that something is said, our question does not make sense. It is a *non sequitur*. A necessary presupposition is lacking. In the present discussion I wish to suggest that, firstly, the currently dominant theory of transformational grammar, which has its roots in American structural linguistics, indulges in the error of asking *how* linguistic units are put together without giving sufficient attention to questions concerning *what* information is being coded. Secondly, that failure to give adequate attention to the use of language to convey information has carried over into theories of second language learning and methods of second language teaching. And thirdly, that the presupposition that language coding involves both complex linguistic forms and complex sets of extra-linguistic information is essential to an adequate theory of second language learning.

[1] This paper has already appeared in *IRAL*, **9** (1971) in an abbreviated form under the title 'Language use and foreign language learning'.

To begin with, let us examine briefly certain tenets of transformational theory from 1957 through 1966. In *Syntactic structures* (1957), Chomsky stated that his grammar was to be a completely formal description of language structure with 'no explicit reference to the way this instrument is put to use' (p. 103). He argued that syntax and semantics were to be strictly separated, saying 'Grammar is best formulated as a self-contained study independent of semantics' (p. 106). Clearly, Chomsky's original thinking was that language was best understood apart from its instrumental use. This thinking reflected the earlier theorizing of Leonard Bloomfield (1933) and Zellig Harris (1947).

In 1963, with the publication of Katz and Fodor's now famous paper on semantic theory, it finally became generally recognized by American linguists that an adequate theory of language would have to deal with meaning. However, Katz and Fodor assumed that the meanings of utterances could be described, independent of the settings in which they might occur. They ruled out consideration of the contexts in which utterances occur by arguing that 'a sentence cannot have readings [i.e. meanings] in a setting that it does not have in isolation' (p. 488). Again, they were attempting to treat language as a self-contained system apart from its actual use. Oller, Sales, and Harrington (1969) have argued to the contrary that an utterance cannot have any meaning in isolation that it could not have in some setting. In other words, sentences have meaning *because* they are used in communication. In order to understand their meaning and their structure, it is necessary to study relationships which hold between the units of language and the extra-linguistic things talked about by speakers of the language. In other words, in addition to asking 'How is it that speakers say what they mean?', we must ask 'What is it that they mean?' In order to answer the latter question, it should be clear that the contexts of utterances are relevant and, in many cases, essential.

Katz and Postal (1964) followed Katz and Fodor (1963) in excluding from consideration the communicative contexts of utterances. Their semantic theory was largely adopted by Chomsky (1965) who continued to argue that it was fruitless to talk about 'a semantic basis for syntax' (p. 78). In Chomsky (1966), it was argued that the study of the relation between linguistic units and extra-linguistic facts is not necessary to a theory of language. It seems that this was a serious error. Unless linguistic theory concerns itself with the relationships which hold between linguistic units and extra-linguistic facts, the basic nature of language will go unexplained. Moreover, if linguistic theory should continue to relate linguistic units only to other linguistic units, it will be plagued by an incapacitating circularity (Oller, Sales, and Harrington, 1969).

The argument in favor of treating language as a medium of communication was well put by Bertrand Russell in his excellent treatise, *An inquiry into meaning and truth* (1940). Russell was voicing a criticism of the viewpoint of certain philosophers of the logical positivist persuasion. His criticism is acutely applicable as a refutation of Chomsky's argument that language should be treated as a self-contained system apart from its communicative function. Russell says (p. 186):

> The purpose of words, though philosophers seem to forget this simple fact, is to deal with matters other than words. If I go into a restaurant and order my dinner, I do not want my words to fit into a system with other words, but to bring about the presence of food. I could have managed without words by taking what I wanted, but this would have been less convenient.

Anton Reichling (1961) has suggested that the very viewpoint which Russell was criticizing here is the historical source of Chomskyan transformational theory. Regardless of whether or not Reichling is correct, it should be clear that language does function to codify information about extra-linguistic entities, relations, desires, etc. Thus, a theory which continues to deal exclusively with relations between linguistic units and other linguistic units cannot hope to achieve adequacy.

This would seem to be the best explanation for the current trend among a few leading transformationalists away from language as a self-contained system, and towards language as a medium of communication. Papers delivered at the 1969 meetings of the Linguistic Society of America and the Chicago Linguistic Society by Ross, Lakoff and Morgan clearly suggest a changing emphasis in transformational theory. Rather than as a system with a syntactic component as the central element, with no input to it (see Fig. 1),[1] current tendency is to view grammar as

---

[1] Here we also encounter indirectly the controversial issues related to the definition of the terms 'competence' and 'performance'. If we assume with Chomsky (1965) that a model of competence need not account for the facts of performance, then a separate performance model seems to be called for. This seems undesirable, however, because it abolishes the original definition of competence – *viz.* the speaker's capacity to use his language. By this definition an adequate model of competence would account for performance, hence

mediating between a highly organized conceptual data set on the one hand and phonetic representation on the other, with inputs and outputs going in both directions (see Fig. 2). The latter model is more consonant with the fact that language is a medium of communication.[1]

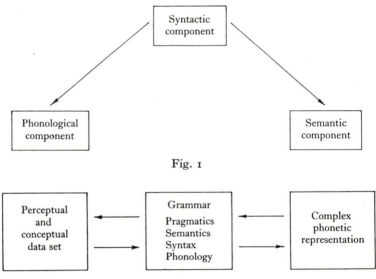

Fig. 1

Fig. 2

At this point, we ask, how does all of this relate to applied linguistics and second language learning? I believe that the question of whether language is essentially a self-contained system or more basically a medium of communication is crucial to theories of second language learning and methods of second language teaching. Suppose we assume

obviating the need for an extra model of performance. See Oller, Sales, and Harrington (1970) for a more complete discussion.

For the alternative viewpoint calling for a model of performance, see Fromkin (1968), and Schwarz (1967).

[1] Incidentally, the latter model conforms more nearly to the thinking of a number of schools of linguistics which have been less popular than the transformational variety. Saussure's lectures a half-century ago (compiled by his students, 1959), the Prague School of Linguistics (see Vachek, 1967), Boas (1911), Sapir (1921), J. R. Firth (1934–51), Reichling (1935, 1961), Hjelmslev's Glossematics (1957), stratificational grammar (Lamb, 1966), Chafe (1965, 1967, 1968), Uhlenbeck (1963, 1967), Rommetveit (1968), and Oller and Sales (1969), all maintain that language must be treated as a medium of communication. Many other works and authors in linguistics and in a great variety of other disciplines could be mentioned.

that language is a self-contained system, going along with transformation-al theory. Our emphasis in theory and practice will necessarily be structural. Clear evidence that linguistic theory has in fact encouraged an emphasis on physical structure, often at the expense of meaning, is found in the vast literature on contrastive studies done at the phonemic, morphemic, and syntactic levels. By contrast there is an extremely sparse literature in applied linguistics on the semantic and pragmatic aspects of language. In fact the study of the pragmatic facts of language – i.e. those having to do with the relations between linguistic units, speakers, and extra-linguistic information – have been almost totally neglected in applied linguistics. Pragmatics, which is the study of linguistic coding, logically includes the study of syntax and semantics. However, it is only recently that this notion has begun to be employed by linguists and psychologists. Interestingly enough, the pragmatic factors involved in the use of language appear to be far more important than phonological and syntactic ones when it comes to matters of speech perception, production, and language learning. (This conclusion finds support in the recent studies of Wason (1961, 1965), Denny (1969), Collins and Quillian (1969), Herriot (1969), and Taylor (1969).)

In terms of application in the classroom, the treatment of language as a self-contained system, apparently encouraged Nelson Brooks (1964), and Rand Morton (1960, 1966) to argue that manipulative skills should be acquired through pattern drills which in themselves are not related to communicative activity. Morton went so far as to insist that the acquisi-tion of manipulative skills must precede expressive use. This is to say that syntactic and phonological structures are best acquired by drill apart from their instrumental use. In an experiment designed to test the relative effectiveness of presenting structures apart from communicative activity and within active communication, Oller and Obrecht (1968) showed that exactly the reverse is true. The mechanical manipulation of structures is best learned in the context of communication.

Another reflection of the assumption that languages are best viewed as self-contained systems, is the common practice by textbook writers of organizing materials on the basis of syntactic principles rather than semantic or pragmatic ones. So many textbooks fall into this category that it would be unreasonable to try to mention even a significant number of them. It seems that the criticism by Otto Jespersen in 1904, against many foreign language textbooks of his day is as apropos as ever in the 1960s. He said (p. 17):

The reader of certain foreign language texts often gets the impression that Frenchmen are strictly systematical beings who one day speak merely in futures, another day in passé définis, and who say the most disconnected things only for the sake of being able to use all the persons in the tense which for the time being happens to be the subject for conversation.

Oller and Obrecht (1969) have shown that sentences are learned more readily when they are placed in a meaningful sequence. In other words, learning is more efficient when the natural order of utterances in communicative events is preserved. The obvious explanation for this fact is that the student is able to capitalize on what he already knows about sentences in a dialogue or story. He has certain expectations about what sorts of information can follow from what has preceded. This frees him in part from concentrating on decoding meanings and allows him to relate meanings to forms.[1]

All of the foregoing supports the assumption that the communicative function of language is an essential point of concern for any theory of second language learning which aims at adequacy. It suggests that the basic principles underlying many current theories of second language learning and practices in second language teaching, may need a thorough re-evaluation. It seems that one of the most important problems for further research and experimentation is the relative importance of syntactic, semantic, and pragmatic factors in second language learning. If contrastive analyses are up-dated to relate *coding* processes in different languages, we may well discover that the most important principles to be considered in program construction are pragmatic ones. A sequence of lessons which are connected in terms of the extra-linguistic information they contain may be superior to a series of lessons linked only by the syntactic principles they illustrate. This is not to suggest that the more familiar syntactic and phonological properties of language should be neglected but rather that perhaps they should be presented in a more realistic context from the point of view of language communication.

It seems that we would do well to reconsider the importance of the

[1] McGeoch and Irion (1952) give the following explanation (pp. 471–2): 'When one says that material A is more readily learned than material B because A is the more meaningful, one implies that A receives more advantage from transfer effects. This, in turn, is tantamount to saying that the learner already knew more about A at the beginning, or possessed more effects of prior training which could be brought to bear on the practice of A.'

relation between the questions 'How is something said in a language?' and 'What is said?' We should be careful to remember that the former question presupposes the latter – that real utterances are *intrinsically* structured for communication.

In conclusion, I would like to make an observation on the present conference. It seems that in spite of the tremendous diversity of viewpoints expressed throughout the meetings of this section of the Second AILA Congress, there has been a certain recurrent theme. The meetings began with the observation by Dr Belasco that 50,000 well-analyzed and well-learned structural items do not insure for the student the capacity to communicate in the target language. He suggested a classroom technique utilizing highly motivating communication in the language. Similarly, Dr Newmark noted the need for the student to observe and participate in realistic use of the language. Dr Sapon even, whose viewpoint is clearly distinct from most of the thinking expressed here, insisted on defining verbal behaviour as an interchange between at least two people. According to him, anything less is not verbal behavior. Professor Asher's developing program stresses a total involvement of the language learner in responses to verbal commands.[1] Dr Carton's considerations on 'inferencing' from extra-linguistic information clearly approach the pragmatic aspects of language communication. Other papers could be mentioned in this regard, but on the basis of these alone, I believe that it is safe to conclude that there is fairly general agreement that the basic goal of foreign language teaching is to enable the student to successfully send and receive messages in the foreign language; that the necessary and sufficient means for achieving this objective is to involve the student in active communication in the target language. The sooner, the better.

BIBLIOGRAPHY

Binnick, Robert I., Davison, Alice, Green, Georgia M., and Morgan, Jerry L. (eds.). *Papers from the Fifth Regional Meeting of the Chicago Linguistic Society*. Chicago: Department of Linguistics, University of Chicago, 1969.
Bloomfield, Leonard. *Language*. New York: Holt, Rinehart, and Winston, 1933.

[1] Professor Asher did not deliver a formal paper at the congress, but presented a film demonstrating his program of teaching by total physical response. Work with this strategy is reported in articles by Asher, and Kunihira and Asher, in *IRAL*, **3** (1965), and by Asher in the *Modern Language Journal*, **50** (1966). [Eds.]

JOHN W. OLLER JR

Boas, Franz. *Handbook of American Indian languages*. Washington, D.C.: Bureau of American Ethnology, Bulletin 40, 1911. Reprinted by Georgetown University Press, 1964.

Brooks, Nelson. *Language and language learning: theory and practice*. 2nd ed. New York: Harcourt, Brace, and World, 1964.

Chafe, Wallace L. 'Meaning in Language.' In Hammel, 1965.
'Language as Symbolization.' *Language*, **43** (1967), 57–91.
'Idiomaticity as an anomaly in the Chomskyan paradigm.' *Foundations of Language*, **4** (1968), 109–27.

Chomsky, Noam. *Syntactic structures*. The Hague: Mouton, 1957.
Aspects of the theory of syntax. Cambridge, Mass.: M.I.T. Press, 1965.
Cartesian linguistics. New York: Harper and Row, 1966.

Collins, Allen M. and Quillian, M. Ross. 'Retrieval time for semantic memory.' *Journal of Verbal Learning and Verbal Behavior*, **8** (1969). 240–7.

Denny, Nathan R. 'Memory load and concept rule difficulty.' *Journal of Verbal Learning and Verbal Behavior*, **8** (1969), 202–5.

Firth, J. R. *Papers in linguistics, 1934–51*. London: Oxford University Press, 1951.

Fodor, J. A. and Katz, J. J. (eds.). *The structure of language: readings in the philosophy of language*. Englewood Cliffs, N.J.: Prentice-Hall, 1964.

Fromkin, Victoria. 'Speculations on performance models.' *Journal of Linguistics*, **4** (1968), 47–68.

Hammel, E. A. (ed.). *Formal semantic analysis*, Special Publication, *American Anthropologist*, vol. 67, no. 5, Pt. 2 (October 1965), 23–36.

Harris, Zellig S. *Methods in structural linguistics*. Chicago: University of Chicago Press, 1951. (Reprinted as *Structural linguistics*, 1961.)

Herriot, Peter. 'The comprehension of active and passive sentences as a function of pragmatic expectations.' *Journal of Verbal Learning and Verbal Behavior*, **8** (1969), 166–9.

Jespersen, Otto. *How to teach a foreign language*. London: Allen and Unwin, 1904. (Reprinted 1956).

Hjelmslev, L., and Uldall, H. J. *An outline of glossematics*. Copenhagen: Travaux du Cercle Linguistique de Copenhague, 1957.

Katz, J. J. and Fodor, J. A. 'The structure of a semantic theory.' *Language*, **39** (1963), 170–210. (Reprinted in Fodor and Katz, *Structure of language*.)

Lakoff, George. 'Selectional restrictions and beliefs about the world.' New York, 1969. Paper delivered at the 43rd Annual Meeting of the Linguistic Society of America.

Lamb, Sydney M. *Outline of stratificational grammar*. Washington, D.C.: Georgetown University Press, 1966.

McGeoch, John A. and Irion, Arthur. *The Psychology of human learning*. New York: Macmillan, 1952.

Morton, F. Rand. *The language lab as a teaching machine: notes on the mechanization of language learning*. Ann Arbor, Mich.: University of Michigan, 1960.
'The behavioral analysis of Spanish syntax: toward an acoustic grammar.' *IRAL*, **4** (1966), 170–7.

Oller, J. W. and Obrecht, Dean H. 'Pattern drill and communicative activity: a psycholinguistic experiment.' *IRAL*, **6** (1968), 165–74.
'The psycholinguistic principle of informational sequence: an experiment in second language learning.' *IRAL*, **7** (1969), 117–23.

178

Oller, J. W., Jr. and Sales, B. Dennis. 'Conceptual restrictions on English: a psycholinguistic study.' *Lingua*, **23** (1969), 209–32.

Oller, J. W., Jr., Sales, B. Dennis, and Harrington, Donald V. 'A basic circularity in traditional and current linguistic theory.' *Lingua*, **22** (1969), 317–28.

'Toward consistent definitions of some psycholinguistic terms.' *Linguistics*, **57** (May 1970), 48–59.

Reichling, Anton. *Het woord*. Amsterdam: North Holland Publishing Company, 1935.

'Principles and methods of syntax: cryptanalytical formalism.' *Lingua*, **10** (1961), 1–17.

Rommetveit, Ragnar. Review of Lyons and Wales, *Psycholinguistics papers*. *Lingua*, **19** (1968), 305–11.

Russell, Bertrand. *An inquiry into meaning and truth*. New York: Norton, 1940.

Sapir, Edward. *Language: an introduction to the study of speech*. New York: Harcourt, Brace and World, 1921.

Saussure, Ferdinand de. *Course in general linguistics*, trans. Wade Baskin. New York: Philosophical Library, 1959.

Schwarcz, Robert M. 'Steps toward a model of linguistic performance: a preliminary sketch.' *MT* (*Mechanical Translation and Computational Linguistics: An International Journal*), **10** (1967), 39–52.

Taylor, Insup. 'Context and structure in sentence production.' *Journal of Verbal Learning and Verbal Behaviour*, **8** (1969), 170–5.

Uhlenbeck, E. M. 'An appraisal of transformational theory.' *Lingua*, **12** (1963), 1–18.

'Some further remarks on transformational grammar.' *Lingua*, **17** (1967), 263–316.

Vachek, Josef. *The Linguistic School of Prague: an introduction to its theory and practice*. Bloomington, Ind.: University of Indiana Press, 1967.

Wason, P. C. 'Response to affirmative and negative binary statements.' *British Journal of Psychology*, **52** (1961), 133–42.

'The contexts of plausible denial.' *Journal of Verbal Learning and Verbal Behavior*, **4** (1965), 7–11.

18   *Fundamentals of language and fundamentals of teaching: the necessity of crossbreeding*

DEAN H. OBRECHT

Every field of applied studies appears to suffer from the same ill effects of becoming involved in the details of development of its contributing disciplines. While the resolution of developmental questions will ultimately shape the applied area, there is very great danger to it in becoming overly committed to the twists and turns or to any particular phase of this development. The ultimate aims of each of the contributing fields are necessarily somewhat different from those of the applied area where they intersect, which has its own objectives.

At the same time, it is folly to fail to consider adequately the nature of the intersection task from the core standpoints of the contributing fields. It is from the special viewpoint occasioned by consideration of the really central issues of these contributors that practitioners in the applied field can profit. However, the applied worker must exercise perhaps his most important feat of judgement in determining what *not* to espouse, which contributory doctrines not to incorporate at all, which developmental controversies to approach cautiously. In short, when operating in the role of applier, he must restrain himself from taking on the special tasks associated with research in one or more contributing areas, and must judge the apparent values of all contributing fields solely by their proven efficacy according to the central criteria and objectives of the *applied* field. It is not directly his job to assess competing theories within the base science. Applied science is not pure science, and is ill served if its own ends are neglected or distorted in the interests of supporting one or another of the competing theories in the science from which it is derived. The base science, of course, is also poorly served if the results of its application are not scanned for inferential evidence leading to evaluation of competing theories and views, with these results feeding back as soon as possible to the base science. The problem is to have the proper person performing the proper evaluation at the proper time, for the correct reasons. For example, linguists have tended to design language teaching materials along lines conforming to their current notions of linguistic structure or theory, sometimes with greater interest in promoting these notions than in carefully researching language teaching effectiveness.

One can undertake a brief survey by dividing contributors to the field of applied linguistics into three categories; structuralists, psycholinguists, and generative grammarians.

I. *Structural linguists*

Structuralists have contributed a great deal to the field of language learning, and have held a particular position of influence in applied linguistics by simply being dominant during the principal development of the latter field. The structuralists helped to introduce, reintroduce and popularize certain crucial views into the language teaching field, as is well known.

Some of the errors and misemphases introduced at the same time are more to be attributed to the newness of applied linguistics and to the paucity of any sensible scholarly support for language teaching notions than to miscues by the structuralists themselves. Positive points first:

(*a*) Positive. A recognition of the systematic nature of language was spread widely by the structuralists, including a keen appreciation of the need for facile control of the structural patterns of language.

(*b*) Positive. Reintroduction of the notion of primacy of spoken language control was effected mainly by structuralists.

(*c*) Positive. A concomitant systematic and *emphatic* approach to phonology was achieved, with results that are frequently a joy to hear.

(*d*) Negative. An *over*emphasis on language as unmotivated recurring structural partial–sames was popularized, leading to the inescapable impression by students and teachers alike of a highly systematic but only trivially extensible code, seemingly immune to developmental or other outside pressures; a system teachable only through a fairly low-level mechanical plateau, only extendable to real-world use through the invocation of an apparently very large level which could only be labeled magic. In particular, syntax was largely ignored, and thus left to the magic level.

(*e*) Negative. By lack of alternative instances of obvious expertise, an overemphasis on phonological perfection was introduced, plus an accompanying overemphasis and overextension of the '-emic' principle, in applied as well as in general linguistics.

(*f*) Negative. Together with and as a result of overemphasis on mechanical manipulation of language patterns, there arose an underemphasis on the practical transmission and reception of information about the real world. An obvious result of this is the horror many of us have felt upon discovering (yet again) that a student who could manipulate pattern changes perfectly had either *no* idea, or worse, a *wrong* idea of what he was saying, and also no idea of when to say it.

II. *Psycholinguists*

The psycholinguists have also contributed specifically to applied linguistics, though as yet in a disappointingly small and specialized way. The application of a psychological learning theory to language teaching is, after all, an applied psychology task, and not a research study in the basic discipline of either psychology or linguistics.

(*a*) Positive. Psycholinguists and psychologists have reminded the field that the language learner is a trainable organism with known mechanisms of habit formation, differential rates of learning, response to various training regimes, etc., and have clearly called attention to the fact that language communication by humans is a behavioral phenomenon, analyzable on a behavioral basis in a real-world setting, and *not* necessarily dependent in the analysis on language structure.

(*b*) Negative. Behavioral psycholinguists, through an excessive theoretical interest in the behavior of the organism have largely failed, as yet, to seek pragmatic knowledge of the actual everyday learning tasks of second language acquisition, especially outside programmed learning experiments. It is ridiculous for linguists to specify training drills and procedures, rather than psycholinguists (though this has been the norm), but only if the psycholinguists know nearly as much about language as the linguists, and nearly as much about learning as the psychologists.

(*c*) Negative. An overly precise requirement of experimental methodology exists, evidently inherited from the parent discipline of psychology, where extreme refinement is necessary in order to detect the very small effects of minute experimental manipulations. Psychology is a highly developed discipline which necessarily operates on fine-grained distinctions. This has apparently made psycholinguists, attentive to the first-named discipline in their multiple-discipline field, excessively cautious and excessively concerned with experimental methodology in approaching second language learning. But the state of development of this enormous field is comparatively so primitive that the need is *not* for such fine-grained experiments, nor for yet another replication, but for extremely basic studies. That is, the need is for experiments specifically in *applied* psycholinguistics (a field in which many reputations both remain and need to be made), devoted to pragmatic language teaching, and not necessarily directly applicable to research in psychology.

III. *Generative grammarians*

The use of the term generative grammarian is dangerous, but any term one selects brands him an idiot in the eyes of one or another contingent of the group to which I wish to refer and to which I must attach a label. (Yes, I know all the other labels!) I have been cheered by hearing of the occasion on which a group of Harvard graduate students held a mock funeral to bury deep structure, upon hearing that it had that day been destroyed. I was even more cheered to hear that they had carefully plotted and preserved the grave coordinates in anticipation of its possible revival.

Naturally, and like all of us, the generative grammarians have assumed that their insights and emphases in language correspond directly to procedures in language learning and utilization. It has been my experience that while the linguistic performance (and competence) of language students can be 'accounted for' and 'described' in structural, traditional, behavioral, or generative terms, none of these approaches is really adequate, especially if rigorously isolated. No single theory, from any field, is yet adequate to account for the daily use of language, much less such special problems as its acquisition and its variety.

(*a*) Positive. The generative grammarians introduced effectively the notion that the task of a language learner is to learn to produce and understand reasonably grammatical utterances in the language. While scarcely novel, this notion arrived on the language teaching scene in time to promote a turn from exclusive consideration of the 'bits and pieces' of language structure to a consideration of the ability to construct and utter whole sentences (even novel ones) in the language.

(*b*) Negative. One fault, though it must be viewed as redressing an imbalance, is an excessive de-emphasis of phonology.

(*c*) Negative. An excessive devotion to the notion of linguistic competence appears to characterize most generative grammarians. It seems clear that, even if somehow less basic, linguistic performance occurs, must be accounted for, and is *not* trivial, no matter what anyone says.

(*d*) Negative. In concert with an unhappiness over the concern with a largely unmeasurable competence, working linguists and language teachers are amused by the notions of at least some of the early generativists, whose theories permit troublesome facts of language use and acquisition to disappear.

(*e*) Negative. Generative grammarians from time to time propose particular linguistic explanations which cannot be faulted as to logic, but which to any experienced teacher appear patently wrong – being, for example, of an order of magnitude in skills of analysis and abstraction totally beyond any operation or level of skill conceivable for any native speaker at the age of his alleged acquisition of the structure or concept involved. A structural explanation which is excessively complex, no matter how logically impeccable, is probably wrong, particularly when of necessity it imputes such an understanding to children, rather than linguists. Generative grammarians tend to ignore the daily use of language by ordinary people in real situations in a noisy world.

(*f*) Negative. Thus it must be said that generativists have suffered by their insistence (which none of them would admit) on the near-exclusive treatment of 'the ideal speaker–hearer', and thus have till now had less impact on applied linguistics than they deserved. No amount of logic and precision can make tolerable the elimination of a variable human talker and human perceiver from the linguistic equation.

How have the doctrines referred to above tied together, and do they really conflict? Further, do they and their points of contact indicate any general trend or approach which may be profitable?

It seems to me that the various contributing fields have each fastened on the aspects of language or language learning that each was best equipped to deal with, and that each has erred in believing its 'special truth' to be fundamental, which it is, and therefore sufficient, which it is *not;* at least to the accomplishment of the announced task. I feel constrained to point out here that I am not attempting to ingratiate myself with any or all of the contributing fields by saying that all their practi-

tioners are good fellows and can no doubt learn to get on with each other
and with their basic research, while maintaining an eye towards the
applied field, permitting it to make its own pragmatic selections and
perform its own research.

Quite evidently, given the differing nature of various tasks involved in
language learning, the individual differences in composition, objectives,
and learning style of the students, various kinds of drill and learning will
be effective. From what I judge to be the non-total possession of
language-learning-truth by any single branch of knowledge, I deem it
quite likely that all the insights and procedures of various sub-fields are
valid and fruitful at one or another stage of language learning, and that
they may often be valid all at the same time, so long as they are not held
to be exclusive. Certainly intelligent instructional programs can be
designed to incorporate the principal discoveries and desiderata of all
these fields, since it is clear that good language teachers have always
combined them and successful language learners have always employed
them. Both, for example, have always perceived that language is used to
transmit and receive information, with all else – including nicety of
pattern and grammaticality or elegance of speech, being subsidiary in the
extreme.

We *know* about pattern practice for habit formation in manipulation
of structural entities. We also know, to our sorrow, that though it works
for habit formation, it is an unqualified disaster when made into a 'total
method' imposed upon our kindly but pragmatic and restive young. We
know that a goal in language learning is to generate and perceive well-
formed sentences. Habit formation is essential to the latter goal, and
therefore they are in no way incompatible, but rather, mutually suppor-
tive. However, we do not have well-founded principles of learning and
training on which to base practical programs designed to induce
learners to possess these abilities *and* to generate correct and fluently
delivered sentences, or to understand them, in direct and appropriate
manners of response to the environment.

Speakers do not simply generate sentences, but generate them in
response to stimuli, which may include other sentences generated in their
hearing. Further, they observe all that which takes place within their
purview both before and after phonation, and their vocal emissions are
altered or determined as a result of their observations. Anyone using
language in the real world is obviously well aware of this mutual effect
between language and environment. Its apparent suspension in other

186

interests during language training is harshly unrealistic, as well as unmotivating.

As early as about thirty-five years ago pilots found themselves concerned with flight simulators, apparently beginning with the Link Trainer, in which they were able to practice instrument flight in weather without pranging expensive aircraft or killing themselves. Flight simulators, now universally used by all airlines, air forces and space programs have reached a stage of sophistication that can be terrifyingly real. Some anguished pilots have dashed themselves ingloriously to the floor attempting to bail out of the things, to the merriment of all others concerned. And these were rudimentary models! The newer, computer-controlled models, complete with audio and visuals, are nothing short of fantastic, and represent a sizeable and knowledgeable industry. It has already been demonstrated that shared-time on-line computer-assisted instruction is not only possible but economically feasible for language instruction. It has further been demonstrated that language laboratories, as a very low-level simulator of actual language experience, have a certain usefulness, if properly controlled and properly integrated into the course of study. It is also true that language laboratories can easily be computer controlled, with great efficiency. I believe that we can and must pull all these representatives of various theories and technologies together.

It is evident that attention to computer-controlled language-learning environmental simulators, which are already economically feasible – in view of high instructional costs, increasing student loads, limitations on faculty size, and so forth – can only be beneficial. Further, such an approach lends itself well to the technical orientation of modern applied linguistics, and would also easily encompass and well serve the theoretical and research interests of all the contributing fields. Demands for attention to individual differences could certainly be met, and a large computer program could supply and usually evaluate all the sorts of activities currently handled in even the best language laboratories. In addition, exciting work on environmental simulation could be added at trivial additional cost. Economic considerations seem non-significant on two grounds: firstly, every nation larger than twelve square miles appears to possess both an airline and one or more gigantic computer installations; and secondly, supplying hardware, rather than additional trained professionals, is cheaper in this world of exploding populations of persons who persist in following nature's rate of maturation. Further, the degree of utilization of any such system would remain optional, while the system could also be programmed to represent any desired mix of teaching concerns, and could be altered at any time – far more easily than can a faculty. The computer is also totally indifferent and impervious to the linguistic or pedagogical philosophies of those directing it, though wholly dependent on them.

Earlier I mentioned that structuralists have been justly criticized for an excessive and finally sterile preoccupation with the bits and pieces of language structure. It appears that in the sense of completeness, of fully motivated concern with the absolute basics of human, voice-powered communication, both psycholinguists and generative grammarians have also been guilty of a 'bits and pieces' approach. Their particular choice of bits and pieces has been different, and all these conglomerations of bits and pieces total nicely to a valuable body of knowledge concerning human communication and language acquisition. The combination, I believe, if the parts are viewed as not mutually exclusive, represents an adequate understanding (while scarcely a coherent theory) to permit us to adopt a pragmatic technological approach. Though I favor 'enormous' simulators which would permit detailed tinkering with the program, both as a research device and in anticipation of future necessity, no such equipment is necessary to the adoption of a multiple-model, strictly eclectic pedagogy, nor to heavily increased efforts to simulate real language use in classroom and laboratory.

19   *A cognition-based program of second language learning*

C. I. C. ESTACIO

The thesis of this paper is that a relationship exists between language instruction and a student's intellectual development, and that a language design which recognizes this relationship can do much towards developing cognitive substructures and repertoires necessary for attaining language proficiency even at very late stages of extensive second language failure.

The vehicle is a pilot project to re-teach English to a linguistically substandard freshman college population at a university in Manila. Aimed at developing literacy in English, the project is a practical measure to repair the damage done by ten years of generally unsuccessful language teaching. A dubious distinction that the Philippines is the third largest English-speaking country after the United States and Britain is countered by the rather reasonable argument that it is also probably the largest nation where English is used badly.

At college level the accumulated effects of second language inadequacies are most felt. Weak in oral expression, students cannot communicate with clarity or precision; poor in reading, they do not profit from the printed page; and deficient in writing skills, they find it laborious to make the simplest reports.

Faced yearly with such a problem, the University of the East, a private institution with an enrolment of over 60,000, representing a wide spread of training and language background, sought a workable remedy. This took the form of a new unit named the Center for Language Education and Research, whose immediate task was to set up a corrective English program for freshmen. The Center, realizing that in problems of method linguistics reasonably disclaims solutions, looked to additional disciplines for contribution.

Testing and other devices at the start of the term revealed, as expected, almost elementary-level skills. Deficiencies and errors in fact covered so many areas that the most sensible step was not to focus on any specific ones but to assume zero-knowledge and start completely over again. Moreover, re-teaching the language simply as a system of habits through repetition and automatizing pattern drills was definitely not the answer. Neither could the teaching items be presented merely in contexts of contrived and usually inflexible dialogues with specific settings. At that late stage, the second language which is both tool and content had to be learned within contexts of fundamental knowledge of lasting value. It had to be, to quote Bruner,[1] 'knowledge of the natural world, knowledge of the human condition, knowledge of the nature and dynamics of society, knowledge of the past so that it may be used in experiencing the present and aspiring to the future, as well as knowledge of the products of (one's) artistic heritage.'

A program which answered the practical needs was available in the English for Television Series developed over the last thirty years by Richards and Gibson and their associates at Harvard. Field-tested in parts of South America and Israel, and earlier, on Japanese, Italians, Greeks and Puerto Ricans, the materials have consistently shown significant positive effects.[2] With necessary modifications in method suited to college-age students, and extensions in content to suit local needs, we hopefully embarked on the project.

RESEARCH METHODOLOGY

No controls were instituted as the situation did not call for comparison with any set of procedures or materials. In current use is an American-prepared text stressing repetition, memorization, and imitation of patterns. For the first time, the Harvard materials were to be used with college retardates and for corrective, rather than initial teaching.

Forty-five heterogeneous groups of 35 to 40 members each, average age seventeen, average IQ 100, followed eight teachers, who had been selected on the basis of their thoughtful replies to a questionnaire on various aspects of language training. The teachers averaged eight years of experience in traditional book method and/or audio-lingual techniques.

[1] Bruner (1962), p. 122.
[2] Cf. Eson (1963).

THE PROGRAM

The origins of this program go back right here to Cambridge University, where I. A. Richards was teaching in the 1930s. In 1939, having gone to Harvard after teaching English in China, Professor Richards started his collaboration with Christine Gibson in the task of improving methods of teaching English as a second language, evolving the techniques now known as the Harvard Graded Direct Method. In Richards' words: the HGDM: that is the *nutshell*. The nut inside is: a way of making the learning of English fully intelligible from the start.

The program consists of forty-eight semantically ordered film lessons teaching concepts of relationship, history, geography, natural events, science and art, using a controlled 500-level vocabulary of high utility. The first twenty-four of these films start with live dialogues, followed by animated captionless cartoon sequences depicting a series of thirty or so related sentences, mediated by a native voice which the class imitates. A second time the cartoons return, now with captions, for reading practice. Film viewing here is not plain audio-visual-lingual exercise, but an exercise in close observation of relationships, as the design encourages active mental comparison of the elements of the depiction (or SIT, short for *situation*), and the elements of the utterances (SEN, or *sentence*). The detailed scrutiny and contrasting of the audio-visual stimuli, moreover, foster needed attentional behaviors which no amount of rule-bound conventional teaching has been able to achieve.

Oral demonstration of new structures follows, then oral application, at which stages students are always actively saying what they are doing. The focus in all the context-situations, whether acted out or pictured, is on objective reality; those for initial lessons, especially, are culled from elements of the universe isomorphic with language, so that awareness that language is rooted in concrete experience is instilled, thereby avoiding early, through verification of utterance reality, usual tendencies towards empty verbalization.

FEATURES

What are some of the features of this program which aims at depth in learning? Among other things, the following:

1. That language learning is a problem-solving activity, and the laboratory or discovery method can effectively be used for it.

2. A structure or pattern underlies all knowledge, and method and material should reflect this fact.

3. The study of language is a study of the interaction of words in context. Words are fluid items, and singly or in combination, they change their meaning from context to context. Language study, in short, should always be a study of meanings.

4. A vocabulary selected on the basis of usefulness is, for second language beginners, to be preferred to words chosen from frequency lists. There are not too many words of high utility, and a small vocabulary that can say much will reduce a beginner's learning load.

5. Depth in language learning may be achieved through good design: the elements of design are grading, sequencing and continuity.

6. One needs language to study language, and the different fields of knowledge must be drawn upon for contribution. As Richards says, 'While you're teaching English, you might as well teach everything else.'

The goals of this program, as I see them, go beyond the merely utilitarian aims of practical discourse. These aims the program does not reject, but on a different plane it stresses the 'valuative' uses a study of language ought to have, the qualities which spell the meaning of true literacy. For this view of language study looks ultimately to an ethical *man* through providing fundamental intellectual and moral equipment which every adult normal person should possess. Language becomes an integrative factor, a means to self-discipline and self-realization.

The main task, always, is to make the learner aware as early, as clearly, and as fully as possible, of what it is he is expected to do. So much failure in any undertaking is due to not having a clear understanding of what the precise problem is, and not being able to inquire because the environment does not foster inquiry. The result is absence or timidity of response, or responses made without benefit of thought or verification.

Simplification is a key feature here. Limit and simplify the task at the beginning if we are to prepare for successful future learnings. Simplification has been shown to lead to success, and success, attained through routes understood all the way, can be its own best reward. Motivation coming from increasing competence rather than extrinsic rewards thus becomes a dominant factor in learning, and leads to further self-learning.

The cognitive psychologist Bruner speaks of two kinds of teaching – what he calls the expository mode and the hypothetical mode. The former would have the teacher as the active participant, the main arbiter, the dispenser of information; the student mainly listens and tries to follow the direction which the exposition takes. In the second type, the teacher and student are on a more or less equal level of participation and collaboration. The teacher does not offer answers; mainly, he incites, he serves as catalyst; the student, on his side, takes active part not only in the problem's solution but in its formulation and in the evaluation of the answer or answers. The first leads to 'convergent' learning, knowing the right answers; the second to creativity.

The hypothetical approach encourages searching rather than waiting to be told. It is the method of discovery – a method of problem-solving, generating that kind of learning which is not mere yielding to insensitive and repetitive pressure from without, but learning through controlled thought – the kind of learning characterized by growth from within.

In the program as we have adapted it at the Center for Language Education and Research, the learner is actively guided by design without express cuing, towards an awareness that there will be something to find, and thus to explore for himself.

How is this guidance made possible? The answer is through rigorous organization of SEN–SITS so that comparison-fields may emerge. A primary principle utilized is *Opposition*. To illustrate from the first SEN–SITS:

I am here   You are there

One sees here a fundamental positional opposition of situation matched by a morphologic opposition in sentence elements. Situation and sentence must be seen in opposition against each other to become meaningful. Taken separately, each will generate only informative-type learning.

Simple basic sentences like 'This is a man' and 'He is here' lead to combinations of the type 'This man is here'. In the semantic area sorting statements like 'A house is a thing. Tables are things. Men and women and boys and girls are persons' provide a start in classification.

The principle of opposition has a corollary. This is the principle of association by similarity. Association is thus of two kinds: by contiguity and by similarity. Contiguity association exemplified in recall and recognition types develops an attitude of 'What's the answer?' On the other hand, similarity–difference association builds up, through a process of comparison, an attitude of 'What's the problem?' Contiguity reproduces, and fosters conformity; similarity explores, is critical, and therefore is constructive. Contiguity-based teaching is likely to generate mere mechanical procedure, and, used beyond reasonable limits, becomes boring and dehumanizing.

EVALUATION

Observed progress, even at the initial stages, has been so encouraging that we now look to statistics and documented experimentation preparatory to adopting the program university-wide. Close-up observations, testing and student comments reveal the following strengths:

1. An impressive growth in ability to talk and write not only grammatically acceptable but meaningful and content-rich sentences in series.

2. Ability in logical sequencing.

3. Sensitivity to one's errors and those of others, and quick correction.

4. Considerable reduction in the number of lapses into native speech patterns, which seems to point to lack of need to translate.

5. Precision and objectivity of statements; transfer is visible in care in judgment-making.

6. A dramatic change from passivity to lively articulateness.

CONCLUSION

We are optimistic about the future. The observed results seem to support the assumption that instruction in language has a direct effect on the development of cognitive processes. A learner seeks meaning in his tasks, and where this is made clear through carefully planned progressions of controlled, integrated phonemic, lexical and syntactic items in contexts of unambiguous denotative discourse, a person develops successful strategies for self-discovery and problem-solving. Training in scientific observation, an ingredient of all scientific enquiry, brings awareness of the connectedness of all knowledge.

Such awareness encourages the process known as 'learning how to learn' and can lead one to the beginnings of an answer to the question – 'What is life for?'

BIBLIOGRAPHY

Bruner, Jerome. *On knowing: essays for the left hand.* Cambridge, Mass.: Harvard University Press, 1962.
Eson, Morris. 'A semantically-sequenced design of instruction.' Mimeo. Albany, New York, 1963.